ART
AND SCHOLASTICISM

With Other Essays

By

JACQUES MARITAIN

Translated by

J. F. SCANLAN

PUBLISHERS' NOTE

The first edition of Art et Scolastique *was translated in 1923 under the title* The Philosophy of Art. *Five hundred copies only were printed, on hand-made paper, at St. Dominic's Press, Ditchling. The present translation has been made entirely afresh from the latest French edition, which has been considerably revised by the Author and has the addition of* The Frontiers of Poetry, An Essay on Art, Some Reflections on Religious Art, *and several new* Notes.

The third of these additions has been kept in its form of a lecture delivered during the *Journées d'Art Religieux* in 1924.

CONTENTS

vii

LIST OF PRINCIPAL NOTES

CONTENTS ix

ART AND SCHOLASTICISM

I

THE SCHOOLMEN AND THE THEORY OF ART

THE Schoolmen composed no special treatise with the title "Philosophy of Art." This is a consequence, no doubt, of the stern discipline of teaching to which the philosophers of the Middle Ages were subjected. They were absorbed in sifting and exploring in every direction the problems of the School and indifferent about leaving unexploited areas between the deep quarries they excavated. There is nevertheless a far-reaching theory of Art to be found in their writings, but it is to be sought in austere dissertations on some problem of logic: "Is Logic a liberal Art?"—or of moral theology: "How does Prudence, at once an *intellectual and moral* virtue, differ from Art, a merely *intellectual* virtue?"

In dissertations of the sort, the nature of art being studied only incidentally, art in general is the subject of debate, from the art of the shipwright to the art of the grammarian and the logician, not the Fine Arts in particular, the consideration of which has no "formal" bearing on the matter under discussion. Recourse must be had to the metaphysics of the Ancients to discover what they thought about Beauty, and a progress thence be made to Art to see what happens when the two terms meet. Disconcerting though it be, such a method nevertheless points a useful moral by drawing our attention to the error in the "Æsthetics" of modern philosophy, which, considering under art the Fine Arts only and dealing with the beautiful only as it concerns art, runs the risk of spoiling the proper conception of both.

A full and complete theory of Art could therefore be composed from the materials prepared by the Schoolmen, if they were collected and worked over again. My present

purpose is merely to indicate a few of the main features of
such a theory, and I beg to be excused the dogmatic form
so imposed upon an unpretentious essay in the hope that,
despite their inadequacy, these observations apropos of
and concerning maxims of the Schools will draw attention to
the utility of having recourse to the wisdom of Antiquity
as also to the possible interest of an exchange of views
between philosophers and artists, at a time when the necessity
of escaping from the vast intellectual confusion bequeathed
to us by the nineteenth century and finding once more the
spiritual conditions of work which shall be *honest* is everywhere felt.

II

THE SPECULATIVE ORDER AND THE PRACTICAL ORDER

THERE are virtues of the mind whose *sole end is knowledge.* They belong to the *speculative* order.

Such are: The Understanding of first principles, which, once we have derived from the experience of our senses the ideas of Being, Causation, End, and the like, makes us perceive at once—through the active light which is in us naturally—the self-evident truths upon which all our knowledge depends; Science, which produces knowledge demonstratively, by attributing causes; Wisdom [1], which makes us contemplate first causes, wherein the mind embraces all things in the superior unity of a simple glance.

These speculative virtues perfect the mind in its peculiar function, in the activity in which it is purely itself: for the object of the mind, as such, is simply and solely knowledge. The mind is active and its action indeed is speaking absolutely, life *par excellence:* but it is an *immanent* action remaining wholly within the mind to make it perfect, and by means of it the mind, with insatiable voracity, seizes hold of being and draws it to itself, eats being and drinks it, so as to "become itself, in a way, all things." The speculative order is therefore its peculiar order: it finds its ease therein. The good or evil estate of the subject, its needs or convenience, are alike indifferent to it: it takes its joy in being and has eyes only for being.

The *practical* order differs from the speculative order because in practice man tends to something other than mere knowledge. If he has knowledge, it is not simply so that he shall rest in truth and enjoy it (*frui*); but rather to put what he knows to some use (*uti*), with a view to making or doing something [2].

Art belongs to the Practical Order. Its orientation is towards doing, not to the pure inwardness of knowledge.

There are, to be sure, speculative arts which are at the

3

same time sciences, e.g. logic: such scientific arts perfect the speculative intellect, not the practical intellect; but the sciences in question retain in their *manner* an element of the practical, and are arts only because they involve *the making of a work*—in this case a work wholly within the mind, whose sole object is knowledge, a work which consists in putting order into our concepts, in framing a proposition or an argument [3]. The result is then, that wherever you find *art* you find some action or operation to be contrived, some work to be done.

III

MAKING AND ACTION

THE Mind as a faculty is a complete self-subsisting whole, but it goes to work very differently according as it has knowledge for the sake of knowing or for the sake of doing.

The speculative intellect will find its perfect and infinitely superabundant joy only in the intuitive vision of the Divine Being: it is through it that man will then possess beatitude: *gaudium de Veritate*. It is very rarely exercised in absolute liberty on this earth except in the case of the philosopher, theologian or metaphysician, or the devotee of pure learning. In the great majority of cases the reason works in the practical order and for the various ends of human actions.

But the practical order is itself divided into two entirely distinct spheres which the Ancients termed Action (*agibile*, πρακτόν) and Making (*factibile*, ποιητόν).

Action, in the restricted sense in which the Schoolmen understood the word, consists in the *free* use (*free* being here emphatic) of our faculties or in the exercise of our free will considered not in relation to things themselves or the works of our hands, but simply in relation to the use to which we put our freedom.

This use depends upon our specifically human appetite or Will, which of itself does not tend to truth, but solely and jealously to the good of man, that only existing for the appetite which fulfils desire or love and increases the being of the subject or stands to the subject in the same relation as itself. This use is good if it conforms to the law governing all human acts and the true end of human life: and if it is good, the man so acting is himself good, purely and simply.

Action is thus ordered to the common end of all human life and it has a part to play in the perfection peculiar to the human being. The sphere of Action is the sphere of Morality or of human good as such. Prudence, a virtue of the practical intellect which keeps Action straight, is wholly confined within the limits of human conduct. Prudence is the queen of the moral virtues, of high lineage and born to command, because Prudence measures our acts in their relation to an ultimate end which is God Himself, the supreme object of love, but she retains nevertheless a savour of misery, because her province is the multitude of necessities, circumstances and occupations, the arena of human suffering, and because she imbues with humanity everything she touches.

As opposed to Action, the Schoolmen defined Making as *productive action*, considered not in relation to the use to which, assuming it, we put our freedom, but simply *in relation to the thing produced* or the work taken by itself.

This action is what it ought to be, is good of its kind, if it conforms to the rules and the end peculiar to the work to be produced: and the result to which it is directed, if it is good, is for the work in question to be good in itself. So Making is ordered to such-and-such a definite end, separate and self-sufficient, not to the common end of human life; and it relates to the peculiar good or perfection not of the man making, but of the work made.

The sphere of Making is the sphere of Art, in the most universal meaning of the word.

Art, therefore, keeping Making straight and not Action, remains outside the line of human conduct, with an end, rules, and values, which are not those of the man, but of the work to be produced. That work is everything for art—one law only governs it—the exigencies and the good of the work.

Hence the despotic and all-absorbing power of art, as also its astonishing power of soothing: it frees from every human care, it establishes the *artifex*, artist or artisan, in a world apart, cloistered, defined and absolute, in which to devote all the strength and intelligence of his manhood to the service of the thing which he is making. This is true of every art; the ennui of living and willing ceases on the threshold of every studio or workshop.

But if art is not human in the end which it pursues, it is human, essentially human, in its method of working. It involves the making of a man's work, stamped with the character of a man: *animal rationale*.

The work of art has been pondered before being made, has been kneaded and prepared, formed, brooded over, and matured in a mind before emerging into matter. And there it will always retain the colour and the savour of the spirit. Its *formal* element, what constitutes it of its kind and makes it what it is, is its being controlled and directed by the mind [4]. If this formal element is in the least degree lacking, the reality of the art becomes correspondingly dissipated. *The work to be done* is merely the matter of art, the form of it is *undeviating reason*. *Recta ratio factibilium:* I will try to translate into English this vigorous Aristotelian and Scholastic definition and define Art as the *undeviating determination of work to be done* [5].

IV

ART AN INTELLECTUAL VIRTUE

To summarise now the teaching of the Schools concerning art in general, considered in the artist or the artisan and as peculiar to him:

1. Art is before all intellectual and its activity consists in impressing an idea upon a matter: therefore it resides in the mind of the *artifex*, or, as they say, it is subject in that mind. It is a certain *quality* of that mind.

2. The Ancients applied the term *habitus* (ἕξις) to qualities of a distinct and separate kind, essentially permanent conditions perfecting in the line of its own nature the subject they inform [6]. Health and beauty are habits of the body, sanctifying grace a (supernatural) habit of the soul [7]: other habits have for subject the faculties or powers of the soul, and as these naturally tend to action, the habits related to them perfect them in their very dynamism, are *operative* habits: such are the intellectual and moral virtues.

We acquire the last-mentioned kind of habit by exercise and customary use [8]; but we must not therefore confuse habit in the present technical sense with the modern meaning of the word, namely, mere mechanical bent and routine: the two are utterly different and opposed [9]. Customary habit, which attests the solid weight of matter, resides in the nerve centres. Operative habit, which attests the activity of the mind, resides chiefly in an immaterial faculty only, in the mind or the will. When the mind, for instance, originally indifferent in regard to any special object of knowledge, demonstrates some truth to its satisfaction, it makes use of its peculiar activity in a certain way, it arouses within itself a quality which makes it proportionate to, and commensurate with, such-and-such an object of speculation, which lifts it up to and keeps it on a level with that object; it acquires the habit of a science. Habits are interior growths of spontaneous life, vital developments which make the soul better in a given sphere and fill it full of a vigorous sap: *turgentia ubera animae*, as John of St. Thomas calls them. And only the living (that is to say, minds which alone are perfectly alive) can acquire them, because they alone are capable of raising the level of their being by their own activity: they so possess, in such an enrichment of their faculties, secondary motives to action, which they bring into play when they want, and which make what is difficult in itself for them delightfully easy.

Habits are, as it were, metaphysical letters patent of nobility, and just as much as inborn talents make for inequality among men. The man with a habit has a quality in him for the lack of which nothing can compensate, as nothing can take its place; other men are defenceless, he is armour-clad, but his armour is the living armour of the spirit.

Habit again, properly so-called, is stable and permanent (*difficile mobilis*) *precisely because of the object* which specifies it; hence the difference between it and mere disposition, as for example opinion [10]. The object in relation to which it perfects the subject is itself unchangeable,—such is, for the habit of Science, the infallible truth of demonstration,— and it is upon this object that the quality developed in the subject *catches*. Hence the strength and the rigidity of habits, their susceptibility,—they are irritated by any deviation from the straight line to their object,—their intransigence,—they are firmly fixed in an absolute: what possible concession could they make?—their boorishness in society. Men of the world, polished on every surface, dislike the man with a habit and his asperities.

Art is a habit of the practical intellect.

3. Such a habit is a *virtue*, that is to say a quality which, triumphing over the original indetermination of the intellective faculty, at once sharpening and hardening the point of its activity, raises it in respect of a definite object to a *maximum of perfection, and so of operative efficiency.* Every virtue being so determined to the utmost of which the faculty is capable [11], and every evil being a deficiency and a weak-

ness, virtue can incline only to good: it is impossible to make use of a virtue to do evil: it is essentially *habitus operativus boni* [12].

The presence of such a virtue in the workman is necessary to the goodness of the work, *for the manner of the action follows the disposition of the agent and, as a man is, so are his works* [13]. For the work in hand to turn out well, there must correspond to it in the soul of the workman such a disposition as will produce between them the sort of congruence and intimate proportion which the Schoolmen termed *connaturality*: Logic, Music and Architecture respectively graft the syllogism upon the logician, harmony upon the musician, and balance of masses upon the architect. Through the presence in them of the virtue of Art, they *are*, in a way, their work before they create it: to be able to form it, they have conformed to it.

But if art is a *virtue of the practical intellect*, and if every virtue inclines solely to the good (that is to say, in the case of a virtue of the intellect, to what is *true*), it necessarily follows that Art as such (Art, I say, and not the artist, whose actions often run contrary to his art) never makes a mistake and involves an *infallible correctness*. Otherwise it would not be a habit properly so called, stable by its very nature.

The Schoolmen debated at length this infallible correctness of art, and more at large the virtues of the practical intellect (Prudence in the sphere of Action, Art in the sphere of Making). How is it possible to make the intellect infallibly true in the domain of the individual and the contingent? They answered by making a fundamental distinction between *the truth of the speculative intellect*, which consists in *knowing*, in conformity with what is, and *the truth of the practical intellect*, which consists in *directing*, in conformity with what ought to be, according to the rule and the proper disposition of the thing to be done [14]; if there can be no *science* except only of what is necessary, if there can be no infallible truth in *knowledge* of what can be other than it is, there can be infallible truth in *direction*, there can be *art*, as there is *prudence*, where contingencies are concerned.

But this infallibility of art concerns only the formal element in the operation, that is to say the regulation of the work by the mind. If the hand of the artist falters, if his tool proves inferior, if what he is working upon gives way, the defect thereby introduced into the result, into the *eventus*, in no way affects the art itself and is no evidence that the artist has fallen short of his art: as soon as the artist, in the act of judgement made by his intellect, determined the rule and proper disposition applicable to the particular case, no error, that is to say no misleading direction, occurred *in him*. The artist who has the habit of art and the quivering hand,

C'ha l'habito de l'arte e man che trema,

produces an imperfect work but retains a. faultless virtue. The same thing may happen in the moral sphere: the event may fail, but the act resolved according to the rules of prudence will none the less have been infallibly direct. Although extrinsically and on the material side involving contingency and fallibility, in itself, that is to say on the formal side and so far as regulation by the mind is concerned, art does not fluctuate like opinion, but is firmly fixed in certitude.

Manual dexterity therefore is no part of art, but merely a material and extrinsic condition; the labour by which the virtuoso who "plays the harp" acquires agile fingers does not increase his art itself or produce any special form; it merely removes a physical impediment to the practice of the art: *non generat novam artem, sed tollit impedimentum exercitii ejus* [15]: art remains entirely by the side of the mind.

4. The better to define its nature, the Ancients compared it to Prudence, which also is a virtue of the practical intellect. By so distinguishing and contrasting Art and Prudence, they laid a finger upon a vital spot in the psychology of human actions.

Art, it has already been observed, is in the line of Making, Prudence in the line of Action. Prudence discerns and applies the means of attaining our moral ends, which are themselves subordinate to the ultimate end of all human life—that is to say, God. It may be described metaphorically as an art, but it is the art of *totum bene vivere* [16], an art which the Saints alone fully possess [17], with supernatural

Prudence and above all the Gifts of the Holy Ghost, which impel them to divine things in a divine *way* and make them act under the very direction of the Spirit of God and His loving art, by giving them the wings of eagles to help them walk upon the earth: *assument pennas ut aquilae, current, et non laborabunt, ambulabunt et non deficient* [18]. Art has no concern with our life, but only with such-and-such particular and extra-human ends which in regard to Art are an ultimate goal.

Prudence operates for the good of the worker, *ad bonum operantis*, Art operates for the good of the work done, *ad bonum operis*, and everything which diverts it from that end adulterates and diminishes it. The moment the artist works well—the moment the Geometer demonstrates—"it makes little difference whether he be in a good temper or in a rage" [19]. If he is angry or jealous, his sin is the sin of a man, not the sin of an artist [20]. Art in no wise tends to make the artist good in his specifically human conduct; it would tend rather for the work produced, if that were possible, itself to make a perfect use in its own line of the artist's activity [21]. But human art does not produce works which proceed to action of their own motion; God alone makes works of that kind, and so the Saints are truly and literally His masterpiece.

Again, as the artist is first a man and then an artist, it is easy to see what conflicts will rage in his heart between Art and Prudence, his character as Maker and his character as Man. Prudence, no doubt, which in all things judges according to particular cases, will not apply the same rules to him as to a ploughman or a tradesman, will not require a Rembrandt or a Léon Bloy to produce works *which pay* in order to assure the material comfort of their families. The artist will nevertheless require a measure of heroism to keep always in the direct line of Action and not to sacrifice his immortal substance to the devouring idol in his soul. The truth is that such conflicts can be abolished only on condition that a deep humility make the artist as it were unconscious of his art, or if the all-powerful unction of wisdom imbue everything in him with the repose and peace of love. Fra Angelico felt no such inner vexation of spirit.

For all that, the pure artist considered in the abstract as such, is something completely unmoral.

Prudence perfects the mind only presupposing that the will is undeviating in its line of human appetite, that is to say in respect of its peculiar good, which is the good of every man [22]: its business is simply to determine the *means* in regard to such-and-such particular concrete human ends already willed: it therefore presupposes that the appetite is well disposed in regard to such ends.

Art, on the contrary, perfects the mind without presupposing the correctness of the will in its own line of human appetite, the ends at which it aims being outside the line of human good. So "the motion of the appetite which spoils the calculation of prudence does not spoil the calculation of art any more than that of geometry" [23]. The act of *using* our faculties (*usus*) depending upon the will in its peculiar dynamism of human appetite [24], it can be easily understood that Art confers only the power of making well (*facultas boni operis*), and not the *habitual practice* of making well. The artist, if he likes, can refrain from using or misuse his art, as the grammarian, if he likes, can commit a solecism; the virtue of art which is in him is no less perfect on that account. According to Aristotle's famous remark [25] (Aristotle, I feel sure, would have liked the fantasies of Erik Satie[1]), an artist sinning against his art is not blamed, if his sin is wilful, as he would be if it were not, whereas a man sinning against prudence or against justice is blamed all the more for sinning wilfully than for sinning unwillingly. On this point the Ancients observed that Art and Prudence both have first to *judge* and then to *command*, but that the chief function of art is only to judge, whereas the chief function of Prudence is to command. *Perfectio artis consistit in judicando* [26].

Prudence, again, having for matter not something to make, some object determined in being, but the pure use to which the subject puts his liberty, has no certain definite paths or fixed rules. Its fixed point is the direct end to which the moral virtues tend and its business is to determine the

---

[1] Fantasies which are bashfulness itself, showing the utmost concern for austerity and purity.

right means. But to attain this end and to apply the universal principles of moral science, its precepts and counsels, to the particular action to be produced, there are no ready-made rules; for the action in question is involved in a tissue of circumstances which give it an individual character and make it every time a really new case [27]. In every particular case[1] there will be a particular way of conforming to the end. It is for Prudence to discover that way, by using paths or rules subordinate to the will (for the will to make its choice as circumstance and opportunity occur), in themselves contingent and not pre-determined but determined with certainty and definitely laid down by the judgement or decision of the Prudent Man, and therefore by the Schoolmen termed *regulae arbitrariae*. Particular in every particular case, the direction given by Prudence is none the less certain and infallible, as has been said before, because the truth of the prudential judgement is considered in relation to the undeviating intention (*per conformitatem ad appetitum rectum*), not in relation to the event; and supposing a second case were to recur or an infinite variety of cases, *identical in every respect* with a given case, *the same direction* ought strictly to be given in all: but there never will be a single moral case absolutely identical with another [28].

Hence it is that no *science* can take the place of Prudence, for science, however casuistically complicated it may be supposed to be, never has any other than general and ascertained rules.

Hence also the absolute necessity for Prudence, in order to fortify its judgement, to have recourse to the manifold, groping exploration which the Ancients termed *consilium* (deliberation, counsel).

Art, on the other hand, whose matter is a thing to be done, proceeds by *certain, definite ways : imo nihil aliud ars esse videtur, quam certa ordinatio rationis, quomodo per determinata media ad determinatum finem actus humani perveniant* [29]. The Schoolmen, following Aristotle, never tire of insisting upon it and make this possession of ascertained

---

[1] Above all when it is a question, for example, of deciding the exact proportion of two virtues which ought to be practised at the same time, firmness and mildness, humility and magnanimity, mercy and truth, etc.

rules an essential characteristic of Art as such. Some observations will be made later on the subject of these fixed rules in the case of the Fine Arts. It will be sufficient for the present to bear in mind that the Ancients dealt with the virtue of Art considered in itself and all its relations, not in any particular one of its kinds, so that the simplest example of art so considered, one in which the generic concept of art is at once realised, had best be sought in the mechanical arts. The proper end of the art of the shipwright or the clockmaker is an invariable and universal end, determined by reason: to enable a man to sail the sea or to tell him the time—the thing to be made, ship or clock, being itself merely a matter to be adapted to such an end. And for that there are fixed rules, also determined by reason, as suitable to the end and to a certain set of conditions.

So the effect produced is no doubt individual, and in cases where the matter of the art is particularly contingent and susceptible of variation, as, for instance, in Medicine or Agriculture or Strategy, Art will find it necessary in order to supply its fixed rules to use contingent rules (*regulae arbitrariae*) and a sort of prudence, will find it necessary also to have recourse to deliberation, to *consilium*. None the less Art by itself derives its steadfastness from its rational and universal rules, not from *consilium*, and the soundness of its judgement derives not from circumstances and events, as is the case with Prudence, but precisely from the certain and determined ways which are peculiar to it [30]. For this reason certain arts can be sciences—practical sciences such as Medicine or Surgery (*ars chirurgico-barbifica* it was still called in the seventeenth century), or even speculative sciences such as Logic.

5. To sum up: Art is therefore *more exclusively intellectual* than Prudence. Whereas the subject of Prudence is the practical intellect *in so far as it presupposes the undeviating will and depends upon it* [31], Art is not concerned with the proper good of the will and the ends it pursues in its line of human appetite; and if it presupposes a certain rectitude of the appetite [32], this is again in relation to some specifically intellectual end. Like Science, it is bound fast to an *object*

(an object to be made, certainly, not an object of contemplation). It employs the circuit of deliberation and
counsel only accidentally. Although it produces individual
actions and results, it forms judgements only adventitiously,
according to the contingencies of circumstance, and so takes
less account than Prudence of the individuation of actions
and the *hic et nunc* [33]. In short, if, because of its matter,
which is contingent, it accords with Prudence more than with
Science, *according to its formal reason and in so far as it is a
virtue* it accords with Science [33b] and the habits of the
speculative intellect more than with Prudence: *ars magis
convenit cum habitibus speculativis in ratione virtutis, quam
cum prudentia* [34]. The Man of Learning is an Intellectual
demonstrating, the Artist is an Intellectual operating, the
Prudent Man is an intelligent Man of Will acting well.

Such are the main features of the Scholastic theory
of art. Not in Phidias and Praxiteles only, but in the village
carpenter and blacksmith as well, the Schoolmen acknowledged an intrinsic development of reason, a nobility of the
mind. They did not consider that the virtue of the *artifex*
lay in strength of muscle or in nimbleness of fingers or in the
rapidity of a chronometrised and taylorised gesture: nor
was it a merely empirical dexterity (*experimentum*), taking
shape in the memory and in the (cogitative) animal reason,
and imitating art: art cannot dispense with such a talent
[35], but it remains extrinsic to art. It was a virtue of the
mind and endowed the humblest artisan with a certain
perfection of the spirit.

In the normal type of human development and truly
human civilisations, the artisan represents the average man.
If Christ willed to be an artisan in an insignificant village,
it was because He wanted to assume the common lot of
humanity [36].

The Doctors of the Middle Ages did not, like so many
of our introspecting psychologists, make town dwellers,
bookworms and graduates the sole object of their studies;
they were concerned also with the mass of mankind. But
even so they did not neglect the study of their Master.
Pondering the art or activity peculiar to the *artifex*, they

pondered the activity which Our Lord chose to exercise throughout His hidden life; they pondered also, in a way, the activity even of the Father; for they knew that the virtue of art is to be predicated peculiarly of God, like Goodness and Justice [37], and that the Son, plying His poor man's trade, was still the image of the Father and of His action which never ceases [38]: *Philippe, qui videt Me videt et Patrem.*

It is interesting to observe that the Ancients in their classifications allotted no separate place to what we call the Fine Arts [39]. They divided the arts into servile and liberal, according as they required corporal labour or not [40], or rather (for such a division, which is more far reaching than one would think, was derived from the very concept of Art, *recta ratio factibilium*), according as the *work to be done* was in one case an effect produced in the matter (*factibile* properly so called), in the other a pure spiritual composition remaining in the soul [41]. Sculpture and painting on that score belonged to the servile arts [42], music to the liberal arts where it had arithmetic and logic for neighbours—for the musician arranges intellectually the sounds in his soul, as the arithmetician numbers and the logician concepts. The oral or instrumental expression, which in the fluid successions of resonant matter transmits compositions thus completed in the spirit, is an extrinsic consequence and a simple means for such arts, and nothing more.

In the powerfully social structure of mediæval civilisation the artist ranked simply as an artisan, and every kind of anarchical development was prohibited to his individualism, because a natural social discipline imposed upon him from without certain limiting conditions [43]. He did not work for society people and the dealers, but for the faithful commons; it was his mission to house their prayers, to instruct their minds, to rejoice their souls and their eyes. Matchless epoch, in which an ingenuous folk was educated in beauty without even noticing it, as perfect religious ought to pray without being aware of their prayers [44]; when doctors and painters lovingly taught the poor, and the poor enjoyed their teaching, because they were all of the same royal race, born of water and the Spirit!

More beautiful things were then created and there was less self-worship. The blessed humility in which the artist was situated exalted his strength and his freedom. The Renaissance was destined to drive the artist mad and make him the most miserable of men—at the very moment when the world was to become less habitable for him—by revealing to him his own grandeur and letting loose upon him the wild beast Beauty which Faith kept enchanted and led after it obedient, with a gossamer thread for leash [45].

V

ART AND BEAUTY

1. St. Thomas, who was as simple as he was wise, defined the beautiful as what gives pleasure on sight, *id quod visum placet* [46]. The four words say all that is necessary: a vision, that is to say an *intuitive knowledge*, and a *joy*. The beautiful is what gives joy, not all joy, but joy in knowledge; not the joy peculiar to the act of knowing, but a joy superabounding and overflowing from such an act because of the object known. If a thing exalts and delights the soul by the bare fact of its being given to the intuition of the soul, it is good to apprehend, it is beautiful [47].

Beauty is essentially the object of *intelligence*, for what *knows* in the full meaning of the word is the mind, which alone is open to the infinity of being. The natural site of beauty is the intelligible world: thence it descends. But it also falls in a way within the grasp of the senses, since the senses in the case of man serve the mind and can themselves rejoice in knowing "the beautiful relates only to sight and hearing of all the senses, because these two are *maxime cognoscitivi*" [48]. The part played by the senses in the perception of beauty becomes in our case enormous and wellnigh indispensable, because our mind is not intuitive like the angelic mind: it can perceive, no doubt, but only on condition of abstracting and discoursing. In man only knowledge derived through the senses possesses fully the intuivity necessary for the perception of the beautiful. So also man can certainly enjoy purely intelligible beauty, but the beautiful whichis *connatural* to man is that which comes to delight the mind through the senses and their intuition. Such also is the peculiar beauty of our art, which works upon a sensible matter for the joy of the spirit. It would fain so persuade itself that paradise is not lost. It has the savour of the terrestrial paradise, because it restores for a brief moment the simultaneous peace and delight of the mind and the senses.

If beauty delights the mind, it is because beauty is essentially a certain excellence or perfection in the proportion of things to the mind. Hence the three conditions assigned to it by St. Thomas [49]: integrity, because the mind likes being; proportion, because the mind likes order and likes unity; lastly and above all brightness or clarity, because the mind likes light and intelligibility. A certain splendour is indeed according to all the Ancients the essential character of beauty, —*claritas est de ratione pulchritudinis* [50], *lux pulchrificat, quia sine luce omnia sunt turpia* [51],—but it is a splendour of intelligibility: *splendor veri*, said the Platonists, *splendor ordinis*, said St. Augustine, adding that "unity is the form of all beauty" [52]; *splendor formae*, said St. Thomas with a metaphysician's precision of language: for *form*, that is to say the principle determining the peculiar perfection of everything which is, constituting and completing things in their essence and their qualities, the ontological secret, so to speak, of their innermost being, their spiritual essence, their operative mystery, is above all the peculiar principle of intelligibility, the peculiar *clarity* of every thing. Every form, moreover, is a remnant or a ray of the creative Mind impressed upon the heart of the being created. All order and proportion, on the other hand, are the work of the mind. So, to say with the Schoolmen that beauty is the *splendour of form shining on the proportioned parts of matter* [53] is to say that it is a lightning of mind on a matter intelligently arranged. The mind rejoices in the beautiful because in the beautiful it finds itself again: recognizes itself, and comes into contact with its very own light. This is so true that they especially perceive and particularly relish the beauty of things who, like St. Francis of Assisi, for example, know that they emanate from a mind and refer them to their Author.

Every sensible beauty, no doubt, implies a certain delight of the eye or the ear or the imagination: but there can be no beauty unless the mind also is in some way rejoiced. A beautiful colour "washes the eye" as a powerful scent dilates the nostrils: but of these two "forms" or qualities only colour is called "beautiful," because being received, as opposed to the perfume, in a sense capable of disinterested knowledge [54], it can be, even through its purely sensible brilliance, an object of joy to the mind. Again, the more highly developed a man's culture becomes, the more spiritual grows the brilliance of the form which ravishes him.

It is important, however, to observe that in the beauty which has been termed connatural to man and is peculiar to human art this brilliance of form, however purely intelligible it may be in itself, is apprehended *in the sensible and by the sensible*, and not separately from it. The intuition of artistic beauty so stands at the opposite pole from the abstraction of scientific truth. For in the former case it is precisely through the apprehension of sense that the light of being penetrates to the mind.

The mind then, spared the least effort of abstraction, rejoices without labour and without discussion. It is excused its customary task, it has not to extricate something intelligible from the matter in which it is buried and then step by step go through its various attributes; like the stag at the spring of running water, it has nothing to do but drink, and it drinks the clarity of being. Firmly fixed in the intuition of sense, it is irradiated by an intelligible light granted to it of a sudden in the very sensible in which it glitters; and it apprehends this light not *sub ratione veri*, but rather *sub ratione delectabilis*, by the happy exercise it procures for it and the succeeding joy in appetite, which leaps out to every good of the soul as its own peculiar object. Only afterwards will it more or less successfully analyse in reflection the causes of such joy [55].

So, although the beautiful is in close dependence upon what is metaphysically true, in the sense that every splendour of intelligibility in things presupposes some degree of conformity with that Intelligence which is the cause of things, the beautiful nevertheless is not a kind of truth, but a kind of good [56]. The perception of the beautiful is related to knowledge, but by way of addition, "as its bloom is an addition to youth"; it is not so much a kind of knowledge as a kind of delight.

The beautiful is essentially delightful. Therefore by its very nature, by its very beauty, it stirs desire and produces love, whereas truth as such only illuminates. "*Omnibus igitur est pulchrum et bonum desiderabile et amabile et diligibile.*" [57]. It is for its beauty that Wisdom is loved [58]. And it is for its own sake that every form of beauty is loved at first, even if later the too frail flesh is caught in the snare. Love in its turn produces ecstasy, that is to say, makes the lover beside himself: an ecstasy of which the soul experiences a lesser form when it is gripped by the beauty of a work of art, and the fullness when it is absorbed, like dew, by the beauty of God.

And of God Himself, according to Denys the Areopagite, [59] one must be bold enough to say that He suffers as it were an ecstasy of love, because of the abundance of His goodness which makes Him give all things a share of His magnificence. But His love causes the beauty of what He loves, whereas our love is caused by the beauty of what we love.

2. The speculations of the Ancients concerning the nature of the beautiful must be taken in the most formal sense and their thought should not be materialised in any too narrow specification. The idea of *integrity* or perfection or complete execution can be realised not in one way only but in a thousand or ten thousand different ways. The lack of a head or an arm is a considerable defect in a woman but of much less account in a statue—whatever disappointment M. Ravaisson may have felt at being unable to *complete* the Venos of Melos. The slightest sketch of Leonardo's or even Rodin's is nearer to perfection than the most finished Bouguereau. And if it pleases a futurist to paint a lady with only one eye, or a quarter of an eye, nobody denies him such a right: all one is entitled to require—and here is the whole problem—is that the quarter eye is all the lady needs *in the given case*.

It is the same with proportion, fitness and harmony. They differ with the object and the end aimed at. Proportions good in a man are not good in a child. Figures constructed according to the Greek or the Egyptian canon are perfectly proportioned in their kind: but Rouault's yokels are also as perfectly proportioned in their kind. Integrity and proportion have no absolute significance [60] and must be understood solely *in relation* to the end of the work, which is to make a form shine on the matter.

Last and most important: this very brilliance of form, the essence of beauty, shines on matter in an infinite variety of ways.[1]

At one time it is the sensible brilliance of colour or tone, at another the intelligible clarity of an arabesque, a rhythm or an harmonious balance, an activity or a movement, or again the reflection upon things of some human or divine thought [60*b*], but above all it is the profound splendour of the soul shining through, of the soul which is the principle of life and animal energy or the principle of spiritual life, of pain and passion. There is also a more exalted splendour, the splendour of Grace, which the Greeks never knew.

Beauty therefore does not consist in conformity to a certain ideal and unchanging type, in the sense understood by those who, confusing the true and the beautiful, knowledge and delight, insist that to perceive beauty man shall discover "by the vision of ideas," "through the material envelope," "the invisible essence of things" and their "necessary type" [61]. St. Thomas was as far removed from this pseudo-Platonism as from the idealist fancy fair of Winckelman and

---

[1] By *brilliance of form* must be understood an *ontological* splendour which happens to be revealed to our minds, not a *conceptual* clarity. There must be no misunderstanding here : the words *clarity, intelligibility* and *light*, used to characterise the part played by *form* in the heart of things, do not necessarily indicate something clear and intelligible *to us*, but rather something which, although clear and luminous *in itself*, intelligible *in itself*, often remains obscure to our eyes either because of the matter in which the form in question is buried or because of the transcendence of the form itself in the things of the spirit. The more substantial and profound this secret significance, the more concealed from us it is; so much so, in truth, that to say with the Schoolmen that form in things is the peculiar principle of *intelligibility* is to say at the same time that it is the peculiar principle of *mystery*. (There can in fact be no mystery where there is *nothing to know*: mystery exists where there is *more to be known* than is offered to our apprehension.) To define beauty by brilliance of form is at the same time to define it by brilliance of mystery.

It is a Cartesian error to reduce *absolute* brilliance to brilliance *for us*. Such an error produces academicism in art and condemns us to such a poor kind of beauty as can give only the meanest of pleasures to the soul.

If it be a question of the " untelligibility " of the work, I would add that if the *brilliance of form* can be apparent in an " obscure " as in a " clear " work, the *brilliance of mystery* can be as apparent in a " clear " work as in an " obscure." From this point of view neither " obscurity " nor " clarity " enjoys any privilege.

David. Beauty for him begins to exist as soon as the radiation of any form over a suitably proportioned matter succeeds in pleasing the mind, and he is careful to warn us that beauty is in a manner *relative*,—not to the dispositions of the subject in the sense in which relativity is understood nowadays, but to the peculiar nature and end of the thing and to the formal conditions in which it is involved. "*Pulchritudo quodammodo dicitur per respectum ad aliquid. . . .*" [62] "*Alia enim est pulchritudo spiritus et alia corporis, atque alia hujus et illius corporis*" [63]. And however beautiful a created thing may be, it may appear beautiful to some and not to others, because it is beautiful only under certain aspects which some discover and others do not see: it is therefore "beautiful in one place and not beautiful in another."

3. If this be so, it is because the beautiful belongs to the order of *transcendentals*—that is to say, of concepts which surpass all limits of kind of category and will not suffer themselves to be confined in any class, because they absorb everything and are to be found everywhere [63*b*]. Like the one, the true and the good, it is *being* itself considered from a certain aspect, it is a property of being: it is not an accident super-added to being, it adds to being merely a relation of reason, it is being considered as delighting, by the mere intuition of it, an intellectual nature. So everything is beautiful as everything is good, at least in a certain relation. And as being is everywhere present and everywhere various, the beautiful likewise is scattered everywhere and everywhere various. Like being and the other transcendentals, it is essentially *analogous*, that is to say it is predicated for divers reasons, *sub diversa ratione*, of the divers subjects of which it is predicated: each kind of being *is* in its own way, is *good* in its own way, is *beautiful* in its own way.

Analogous concepts are properly predicable only of God, in whom the perfection they describe exists in a "formal-eminent" manner, in a pure and infinite state. God is their "sovereign analogue" [64], and they are to be found in things only as a scattered and prismatised reflection of the face of God [65]. So Beauty is one of the divine attributes.

God is beautiful. He is the most beautiful of beings, because, as Denys the Areopagite and St. Thomas explain [66], His beauty is without alteration or vicissitude, without increase or diminution: and because it is not like the beauty of things, which have all a particularised beauty, *particulatam pulchritudinem, sicut et particulatam naturam*, He is beautiful by Himself and in Himself, absolutely beautiful.

He is exceedingly beautiful (*superpulcher*), because there is pre-existent in a super-excellent way in the perfectly simple unity of His nature the fountain of all beauty.

He is beauty itself, because He imparts beauty to all created beings, according to the peculiar nature of each, and because He is the cause of all harmony and brightness. Every form indeed, that is to say every light, is "a certain irradiation proceeding from the first brightness," "a participation in the divine brightness." And every consonance or harmony, every concord, every friendship and union of whatever sort between creatures, proceeds from the divine beauty, the primitive, super-eminent type of all consonance, which gathers all things together and calls them to itself, well deserving on that account "the name of καλός, which derives from calling." Thus "the beauty of the creature is nothing but a similitude of the divine beauty shared among things," and on the other hand, every form being a principle of being and every consonance or harmony being a preservation of being, the divine beauty must be said to be the cause of being in everything which is. *Ex divina pulchritudine esse omnium derivatur* [67].

In the Trinity, St. Thomas goes on to say [68], the title Beauty is specially appropriated to the Son. As for integrity or perfection, He has truly and perfectly in Himself, without the least diminution, the nature of the Father. As for due proportion or consonance, He is the express image of the Father, a perfect likeness; and it is proportion which befits the picture as such. As for brilliance, He is the Word, the light and splendour of the mind, "perfect Word, lacking nothing and, so to speak, art of the Almighty God" [69].

Beauty therefore belongs to the transcendental and metaphysical order. For this reason it tends of itself to carry the soul beyond creation. Of the instinct for beauty, the *accursed poet* to whom modern art owes the recovery of the consciousness of the theological quality and the tyrannical spirituality of beauty, says, "it is that immortal instinct for the beautiful which makes us consider the world and its pageants as a glimpse of, a *correspondence* with, Heaven. The insatiable thirst for everything beyond, which life reveals, is the liveliest proof of our immortality. It is at once by poetry and *through* poetry, by music and *through* music that the soul perceives what splendours shine behind the tomb; and when an exquisite poem brings tears to the eyes, such tears do not argue an excess of enjoyment but rather attest an irritation of melancholy, some peremptory need of the nerves, a nature exiled in the imperfect which would fain possess immediately, even on this earth, a paradise revealed" [70].

4. Once we touch a transcendental, we touch being itself, a likeness of God, an absolute, all that ennobles and makes the joy of life: we enter the realm of the spirit. It is remarkable that the only real means of communication between human creatures is through being or some one of the properties of being. This is their only means of escape from the individuality in which they are enclosed by matter. If they remain on the plane of their sensible needs and their sentimental selves they tell their stories to one another in vain; they cannot understand each other. They watch each other and cannot see, each infinitely alone, however closely work or the pleasure of love may bind them together. But once touch the good and Love, like the Saints, or the true, like an Aristotle, or the beautiful, like a Dante, a Bach or a Giotto, then contact is established and souls communicate. Men are only really united by the spirit: light alone gathers them together, *intellectualia et rationalia omnia congregans, et indestructibilia faciens* [71].

Art in general tends to make a work. But certain arts tend to make a work of *beauty* and thereby differ essentially from all the rest. The work which involves the labour of all the other arts is itself ordered to the service of man and is therefore a mere means: it is completely enclosed in a definite material *genus* or kind. The work which involves the labour of the Fine Arts is ordered to beauty: in so far as it is beautiful it is an end, an absolute, self-sufficient; and if, as work to be done, it is material and enclosed in a kind, as beautiful it belongs to the realm of the spirit and dives deep into the transcendence and the infinity of being.

The Fine Arts therefore stand out in the *genus* art as man stands out in the *genus* animal. And like man himself they are like a horizon where matter comes into contact with spirit. They have a spiritual soul. Therefore they have many distinctive properties. Their association with the beautiful modifies in their case certain characteristics of art in general, notably, as I shall endeavour to show, all that concerns the rules of art. On the other hand it emphasises and carries to a kind of excess other generic characteristics of the artistic virtue, above all its intellectual character and its resemblance to the speculative virtues.

There is a curious analogy between the Fine Arts and wisdom. Like wisdom, they are ordered to an object transcending man and of value in itself, whose fullness is without limit, for beauty is as infinite as being. They are disinterested, pursued for their own sake, truly noble because their work considered in itself is not made to be used as a means, but to be enjoyed as an end, being a true fruit, *aliquid ultimum et delectabile*. Their whole value is spiritual and their manner of being is contemplation. For if contemplation is not their activity, as it is the activity of wisdom, their object is nevertheless to produce an intellectual delight, that is to say a kind of contemplation, and they also pre-suppose in the artist a kind of contemplation, whence the beauty of the work ought to overflow. For this reason there may be applied to them, due allowance being made, the comparison drawn by St. Thomas between wisdom and games [72]: "The contemplation of wisdom is rightly compared with games for two things to be found in games. The first is that games give pleasure and the contemplation of wisdom gives the very greatest pleasure, according to what Wisdom says of itself in Ecclesiasticus: *My spirit is sweet above honey.* The second is that the movements in games are not contrived to serve another end but are pursued for their own sake. It is the same with the delights of wisdom. . . . Hence divine Wisdom compares its delight to games: *I was with him forming all things and was delighted every day, playing before him at all times : playing in the world*" [73].

But Art remains always essentially in the sphere of Making and it is by drudgery upon some matter that it aims at rejoicing the spirit. Hence for the artist a strange and pathetic condition, the very image of man's condition in the world, where he is condemned to wear himself out among bodies and live with minds. Although he reproaches the old poets for making the Divinity jealous, Aristotle admits that they were right in saying that to the Divinity alone is reserved the possession of wisdom as His true property: "The possession of it is beyond human power, for human nature in many ways is in bondage" [74]. So the production of beauty belongs to God alone as His true property. And if the condition of the artist is more human and less exalted than that of the wise man, it is also more discordant and painful, because his activity is not wholly confined within the pure immanence of spiritual operations and does not consist in itself of contemplating, but of making. Unable to enjoy the substance and the peace of wisdom, he is caught by the harsh exigencies of the mind and the speculative life and condemned to every servile misery of temporal practice and production.

5. "Dear brother Leo, God's little beast, if a minor friar were to speak the language of the angels and raise to life a man already four days dead, write it well that even in so doing perfect joy is not to be found . . ."

Even if the artist were to compass in his work all the light of the sky and all the grace of the first garden, he would not have perfect joy, because he is on the tracks of wisdom and running upon the scent of its perfumes, but never possesses it. Even if the philosopher were to know every reason susceptible of comprehension and every virtue of being, he would not have perfect joy, because his wisdom is human. Even if the theologian were to know every analogy of the divine processions and every motive of Christ's actions, he would not have perfect joy, because his wisdom, though it has a divine origin, is of a human fashion and speaks with a human voice.

Sweet voices, die, . . . dying indeed you are!

The Poor and the Peaceful alone have perfect joy because they have wisdom and contemplation *par excellence*, in the silence of created things and in the voice of Love: united without intermediary to subsisting Truth, they know "the sweetness God gives and the delicious taste of the Holy Ghost." [75]. Hence the exclamation of St. Thomas, shortly before his death, with reference to his unfinished *Summa*: "What rubbish it is! *mihi videtur ut palea.*" And the Parthenon and Our Lady of Chartres, the Sistine Chapel and the Mass in B minor are also rubbish, destined to be burned on the Last Day. "Created things have no savour."

The Middle Ages knew such order. The Renaissance shattered it. After three centuries of infidelity, Art, the prodigal, would fain have become the ultimate end of man, his Bread and Wine, the consubstantial mirror of beatific Beauty. In reality it has only squandered its substance. And the poet hungering for beatitude who asked of Art the mystic fullness which God alone can give could find his only outlet in *Sigê l'abîme*. Rimbaud's *silence* denotes perhaps the end of an age-old apostasy. At all events it clearly indicates that it is folly to try to find in art the words of eternal life and rest for the human heart: and that the artist, if he is not to shatter his art or his soul, must simply be, as artist, what art would have him be—a good workman.

But now the modern world, which had promised the artist all things, will soon scarcely leave him even the bare means of subsistence. Founded upon the two *unnatural* principles of the *fecundity of money* and the *finality of the useful*, multiplying its needs and servitudes without any possibility of there ever being a limit, ruining the leisure of the soul, withdrawing the material *factibile* from the control which proportioned it to the ends of the human being, imposing on man its puffing machinery and its speeding up of matter, the modern world is shaping human activity in a properly inhuman way, in a properly devilish direction, for the ultimate end of all this frenzy is to prevent man from remembering God,

> *dum nil perenne cogitat,*
> *seseque culpis illigat.*

He must consequently, if he is to be logical, regard as useless, and therefore despicable, everything which for any reason bears the mark of the spirit.

"An aristocracy in the order of deeds, but a truly democratic barbarism of the mind, is the portion of the time to come; the dreamer, the man of speculative mind, will be able to maintain his place only at the expense of his security and comfort; jobs, success, or glory will reward the versatility of the mountebank: more than ever, to a degree unknown in the iron age, the hero and the saint will pay for their pride in poverty and loneliness" [76].

Persecuted like the wise man and almost like the Saint, the artist will perhaps recognise his brethren at last and find his vocation once again: for in a way he is not of this world, being, from the moment he begins working for beauty, on the road which leads upright souls to God and makes invisible things clear to them by visible. However few they may then be who will disdain to gratify the Beast and turn with the wind, in them, for the simple reason that they will be exercising a *disinterested* activity, the human race will live.

VI

THE RULES OF ART

The whole formal element of Art consists in the *regulation* it impresses upon matter. And a code of ascertained rules, *viae certae et determinatae*, is, according to the Ancients, of the essence of art.

1. The expression "ascertained rules" conjures up evil memories: we think of the three unities and the "rules of Aristotle." But it is from the Renaissance with its superstitious reverence for antiquity and its dummy Aristotle, not from the Christian Aristotle of our Teachers, that the rigid rules of the grammarians of the *grand siècle* derive. The "ascertained rules" of the Scholastic philosophy are not conventional imperatives imposed upon Art from without, but the high concealed ways by which Art itself, the working reason, goes to work [77]. And every artist is well aware that if this intellectual form ceased to dominate his matter, his art would be a mere sensual confusion [78]. Some words of explanation here seem necessary.

2. First with regard to Art in general, the mechanical and servile no less than the Fine and Liberal Arts, it is important to realise that the rules in question are in fact worthless unless they are in a live spiritual state on a *habit* or virtue of the intelligence, which is the specific virtue of art.

With the *habit* or virtue of art exalting his spirit from within, the artist is a master *making use of* the rules to serve his ends; it is as foolish to conceive him as the "slave" of the rules as to consider the workman the "slave" of his tools. Properly speaking, he possesses and is not possessed by them: he is not *held* by them, it is he who *holds*, through them, matter and reality; and sometimes, in the high moments when the working of genius in art resembles the miracles of God in nature, he will not act against the rules,

but outside and above them, in conformity with a higher
rule and a hidden order. In this sense we must understand
Pascal's remark: "True eloquence laughs at eloquence,
true morality laughs at morality, to laugh at philosophy is
true philosophy," and with it, this racy comment by the most
tyrannical, the most extreme radical, of academic principals:
"Unless you don't give a damn for painting, painting won't
give a damn for you" [79].

There is, as has been said before, a fundamental incom-
patibility between *habits* and egaliterianism. The modern
world has a hatred of *habits* of whatever kind and a very
interesting *History of the Progressive Expulsion of Habits
by the Modern Revolution* might be written. It would go
pretty far back into the past. We should see theologians
like Duns Scotus—"a fish always rots first at the head,"—
and Occam and even Suarez begin by illtreating the most
aristocratic of those queer creatures, the gifts of the Holy
Ghost—not to mention the infused moral virtues. Then the
turn of the theological virtues and sanctifying grace comes
to be filed and planed by Luther and the Cartesian theologians. Natural *habits* receive attention in the meantime;
Descartes, with his passion for levelling, falls foul even of
the *genus generalissimum* to which the unfortunates belong,
and denies the real existence of qualities and accidents.
The whole world at the time is agog with excitement about
calculating machines, everybody dreaming of method.
And Descartes conceives method as an infallible and easy
means of bringing to truth "those who have never been to
school" and people of quality [80]. Leibniz at last invents
a system of logic and a language whose most wonderful
characteristic is to make *thinking unnecessary* [81]. We
then reach the spiritual acephaly of the age of enlighten-
ment.

So *method* or .rules, considered as a *collection of self-
adjusting formulæ and processes, an orthopædic and mechanical
truss for the mind*, tend throughout the modern world to
take the place of *habits*, because a method is open to everybody whereas habits are reserved for the few. Now access
to the supreme joys cannot be allowed to depend upon

a virtue which a few possess and the rest not; therefore beautiful things must be made easy.

Χαλεπὰ τὰ καλά. The Ancients thought that truth was difficult and beauty difficult, that the way was narrow; and that to overcome the difficulty and the altitude of the object, it was absolutely necessary to develop in that subject an intrinsic force and elevation: that is to say a *habit*. The modern conception of method and rules would have seemed to them therefore an outrageous absurdity. According to their principles, rules are of the essence of art, but on condition of forming a habit, a living rule. Without that, rules mean nothing. Stick the consummate theoretical knowledge of all the rules of art upon an industrious graduate working fifteen hours a day but without a shoot of habit sprouting in him, and you will never make him an artist; he will always remain infinitely farther removed from art than the child or the savage with a simple natural gift. So much by way of apology for the too simple-minded or too sophisticated worshippers of negro art.

For the modern artist the problem is absurdly situated between the senility of academic rules and the primitiveness of the natural gift: in the former art has ceased to exist, in the latter it has not yet come into being, except potentially. Art exists only in the living intellectuality of the *habit*.

3. In our time the *natural gift* is lightly taken for art itself, especially if it be disguised in clever faking and a voluptuous medley of colours. Now a natural gift is merely a pre-requisite condition of art, or again a rough sketch (*inchoatio naturalis*) of the artistic habit. Such an innate disposition is clearly indispensable; but without a culture and a discipline, which the Ancients considered should be long, patient and honest, it will never turn into art properly so-called. Art therefore is the product of a spontaneous instinct like love and ought to be cultivated like friendship: because it is a virtue like friendship.

St. Thomas would have us observe that the natural dispositions which differentiate individuals have their root

in the complexion of the body [82]; they concern our
sensitive faculties, particularly the imagination, the chief
purveyor of art, which thus seems to be the *gift par excellence*
which makes the born artist. The poets gladly make it their
principal faculty, because it is so intimately bound up with
the activity of the creative intellect as not easily to be distinguished from it in the concrete. But the virtue of art is a
perfection of the spirit: and it impresses the human being
with an incomparably deeper character than natural dispositions.

The manner of cultivating natural dispositions by education may sometimes atrophy the spontaneous gift instead
of developing the habit, especially if the manner is material,
and rotten with tips and dodges,—or again if it is theoretical
and speculative instead of being *practical*, for the practical
intellect, upon which the rules governing the arts depend,
proceeds by putting an effect into being, not by proving or
demonstrating: and frequently those who know best the rules
of an art are the least capable of formulating them. From this
point of view the substitution (initiated by Colbert and
completed by the Revolution) of academic teaching in
schools for apprenticeship in a corporation is regrettable
[83]. Precisely because art is a virtue of the practical intellect,
the naturally appropriate method of teaching it is education
by apprenticeship, a working novitiate under a master and in
face of reality, not lessons doled out by teachers: and in
truth, the bare idea of an *Academy of fine Arts*, especially
in the sense given to it by the modern State, is as stupid in
conception as the idea of an *Advanced Course of Virtue*.
Hence the revolt of Cézanne and his followers against the
Academy and teachers, a revolt directed, in reality, mainly
against a barbarous system of artistic education.

Art, nevertheless, being an intellectual habit, necessarily
and at all times presupposes such a *formation* of the spirit as
will put the artist in possession of definite rules for working.
In exceptional cases, no doubt, the individual effort of the
artist, of a Giotto [84] for example, or a Moussorgsky, is
itself sufficient to acquire such a formation: and it may even
be said in respect of the most spiritual element in art—
the synthetic intuition, the conception of the work to be done

—that as this depends upon the *via inventionis* or the effort to invent, which needs solitude and cannot be learned from anyone, the artist, where the fine point and highest expression of his art are concerned, forms and educates himself alone: the nearer one gets to the spiritual point of art, the more the *viae determinatae* to be followed will be appropriate and personal to the artist, and as such discoverable by one alone [85]. It may be that nowadays when we suffer so cruelly from all the evils of anarchy, we run the risk of deceiving ourselves as to the nature and extent of the results to be expected from a return to craft traditions.

Be that as it may, for the great bulk of rational and discursive work which art involves, the tradition of a discipline and an education by masters and the continuity in time of human collaboration, in short, the *via disciplinae*, is absolutely necessary, whether it be a question of technique properly so called and material means, or the whole concepted and rational replenishing which certain of the arts (above all in classical times) require and carry along with them: or lastly, the absolutely indispensable maintenance of a sufficiently high level of culture in the average of artists and artisans, everyone of whom it would be absurd to ask to be an "original genius" [86].

To have the thought of St. Thomas in its entirety [87], it must be added that in every form of discipline and teaching the master merely gives assistance from outside to the principle of immanent activity within the pupil. Teaching from this point of view returns to the great conception of *ars co-operativa naturae*. Whereas certain arts attack their matter in order to conquer it, to impose upon it a form which it has only to receive—the art of a Michelangelo, for example, torturing marble like a tyrant—others, because their matter is nature itself, devote themselves to their matter to serve it, to help it attain a form or a perfection to be acquired only by the activity of an interior principle: such are the arts which "co-operate with nature," with the corporal nature, like medicine, with the spiritual nature like teaching (also the art of directing consciences). They operate only by providing the interior principle inside the subject with the means and assistance it requires to produce its effect. It is the *interior principle*, the intellectual light present in the pupil which is in the acquisition of science and art, the *cause* or *principal agent*.

4. If it be a question thereafter of the Fine Arts in particular, their contact with being and the transcendentals creates for them, as far as the rules of art are concerned, a quite peculiar condition.

They are in the first place subject to a law of renewal, therefore of change, unknown, at any rate for the same reason, to the other arts.

Beauty has an infinite amplitude, like being. But the work as such, realised in matter, is in a certain kind, *in aliquo genere*: and it is impossible for a kind to exhaust a transcendental. Over and above the artistic kind to which a particular work belongs, there is always an infinity of ways in which it can be *beautiful*.

There is therefore a sort of conflict to be observed between the transcendence of beauty and the material narrowness of the work to be done, between the formal reason of beauty, the splendour of being and all the transcendentals together, and the formal reason of art, the undeviating activity of manufacturing works to be done. No form of art, however perfect, can encompass beauty in itself as the Virgin contained her Creator. The artist is faced with a vast expanse of lonely sea "without a mast or fertile isle," and the mirror he holds up to it is no bigger than his own heart.

The creator in art is he who discovers a *new typeanalogy* [88] of the beautiful, a new way in which the brilliance of form can be made to shine upon matter. The work he is engaged upon, which, as such, is of a certain kind, henceforth belongs to a new kind and require new rules—I mean a new adaptation of the first and eternal rules [89], and even the use of *viae certae et determinatae* not hitherto employed, which are at first disconcerting.

At that moment the contemplative activity in contact with the transcendental, which constitutes the proper life of the arts of the beautiful and their rules, is plainly predominant. But when artists devote themselves merely to exploiting what has once been discovered it almost necessarily

follows that talent, cleverness, sheer technique, the merely
operative activity peculiar to the *genus* art should gradually
gain the upper hand; rules which were once living and spiritual
will then become material, and that form of art end by exhaust-
ing itself. A renewal will be necessary. Heaven grant that a
genius may be found to achieve it! Even so the change
will perhaps lower the general level of art; it is nevertheless
the very conditions of its life and of the production of great
works [90]. We may believe that from Bach to Beethoven
and from Beethoven to Wagner art has suffered a decline in
quality, spirituality and purity. But would anyone be bold
enough to say that any one of these men was less necessary
than the other? If they load their art with exotic riches
too heavy for any but themselves to bear, the most potent
of them are sometimes the most pernicious. Rembrandt is a
bad master; would any man refuse him his affection?
Even at the risk of painting's being wounded, it was better
that Rembrandt should have played and won, made his
miraculous breach in the invisible world. It is perfectly
true that there is no necessary progress in art [90*b*], that
tradition and discipline are the true nurses of orginality;
and that the feverish acceleration which modern individualism, with its frenzy for revolution in the mediocre, imposes
upon the succession of art forms, abortive schools, and
puerile fashions is the symptom of a far-spread intellectual
and social poverty. Novelty nevertheless is fundamentally
necessary to art, which, like nature, goes in seasons.

5. Art, unlike Prudence, does not presuppose a rectification of the appetite, that is to say of the power of willing
and loving, in relation to the end of man or in the moral
sphere [91]. It presupposes nevertheless, as Cajetan explains
[92], that the appetite should tend directly *to the proper
end of art*. "The truth of the practical intellect is to be
understood not according as it conforms with the object, but
according as it conforms with the direct appetite"—this
principle rules alike the sphere of Making and the sphere of
Action.

In the case of the Fine Arts, the general end of the art is
beauty. But there the work to be done is not merely matter

to be ordered to that end, like making a clock to the end of
telling the time or building a ship to the end of crossing the
water. Being a kind of individual and original realisation
of beauty, the work which the artist is going to do is for him
an end in itself: not the general end of his art, but the particular end dominating his present activity, the end in
relation to which every means must be regulated. Now,
suitably to *judge* such an individual end, that is to say to
conceive the work to be done [93], reason alone is not
sufficient. A *good disposition of the appetite* is necessary, for
everyone judges his particular ends by what he himself actu-
ally is: "as a man is, so does the end appear to him" [94].
The conclusion is that in the case of the painter, the poet and
the musician, the virtue of art, which resides in the intellect,
must not only overflow into the sensitive faculties and the
imagination, but also require the artist's whole appetitive
faculty, his passions and his will, to be rectified in relation
to the end of his art. If every faculty of desire and emotion
in the artist is not fundamentally rectified and exalted in
the line of beauty, whose transcendence and immateriality are
superhuman, human life, the humdrum activity of the
senses, and the routine of art itself, will degrade his conception. The artist must be in love, must be in love with *what
he is doing*, so that his virtue becomes in truth, St. Augustine's phrase [95], *ordo amoris.* so that beauty becomes
connatural to him, bedded in his being through affection,
and his work proceeds from his heart and his bowels as from
his lucid mind. Such undeviating love is the supreme rule.

But love presupposes intelligence; without it love can do
nothing, and, intending to the beautiful, love tends to what
can delight the mind.

6. Lastly, because in the case of the Fine Arts the work to
be done is, so far as it is beautiful, an end in itself, and
because such an end is something absolutely individual,
utterly unique, the artist has every time a fresh and unique
way of conforming to the end, and so regulating the matter.
Hence a remarkable analogy between the Fine Arts and
Prudence.

Art, no doubt, always keeps its *viae certae et determinatae,* and the proof is that all the works of one artist or one school are stamped with the same certain and determined characteristics. But it is with prudence, *eubulia*, good sense, and perspicacity, circumspection, precaution, deliberation, and industry, memory, foresight, intelligence and divination— by using the rules of prudence, not determined beforehand but established according to the contingency of particular circumstances, in a manner ever novel and unpredictable— that the artist applies the rules of his art: on this condition only will it be infallibly regulated. "A picture," said Degas, "requires as much rascality, malice and perversity as the perpetration of a crime" [96]. For different reasons, and because of the transcendence of their object, the Fine Arts thus partake, like hunting or the military art, of the virtue of government.

Such artistic prudence, such a kind of spiritual sensibility in contact with matter, corresponds in the operative order to contemplative activity and the proper life of art in contact with the beautiful. As the rules of the Academy become predominant, the Fine Arts revert to the generic type of art and its inferior species, the mechanical arts.

VII

THE PURITY OF ART

"What we now seek from art," Émile Clermont observed, "the Greeks sought from something quite different, sometimes from wine, most often from the celebration of their mysteries: a frenzy, an intoxication. The great Bacchic madness of these mysteries is what corresponds to our highest degree of emotional exaltation in art, an importation from Asia. But for the Greeks art was altogether different . . . [98]. Its effect was not an upheaval of the soul but a purification, the exact opposite: 'art purifies the passions,' according to Aristotle's familiar and generally misinterpreted observation. And what we need first of all, no doubt, is to purify the idea of beauty. . . ."

1. From the point of view of *art* in general as from the point of view of *beauty*, it is the mind, the Masters of the School perpetually insist, which takes first place in the work of art. They never weary of reminding us that the *first principle of the human work is reason* [99]. Let it be added that in making Logic the liberal art *par excellence*, and in a sense the chief type-analogy to art, they show that in every art there is as it were a vivid experience of Logic.

> *There all is ORDER and beauty,*
> *Richness, tranquillity and voluptuousness.* [100]

If unnecessary stucco is ugly in architecture, it is because it is illogical [100b]: if make-belief and illusion, irritating in general, become simply detestable in sacred art, it is because it is profoundly illogical to make use of deceit for the decoration of God's house [101]: *Deus non eget nostro mendacio*. "The ugly in art," said Rodin, "is the fake, whatever grins at you without cause, senseless affectations, pirouettes and capers, mere travesties of beauty and grace, whatever tells a lie" [102]. "I want you," Maurice Denis adds [103], "to paint your people *so that they look as though*

they were painted, subject to the laws of painting, and don't
let them try to deceive my eye or my mind: the truth of art
consists in the conformity of the work to its means and end."
Which comes to saying with the Ancients that the truth of
art is taken to be *per ordinem et conformitatem ad regulas
artis* [104], to saying that every work of art must be logical.
Therein lies its truth. It must be steeped in logic; not in the
pseudo-logic of clear ideas [105], not in the logic of knowledge and demonstration, but in the working logic of every
day, eternally mysterious and disturbing, the logic of the
structure of the living thing, and the intimate geometry of
nature. Our Lady of Chartres is as much a marvel of logic
as the *Summa* of St. Thomas: flamboyant Gothic itself is
opposed to stucco, and the richness of ornament in which it
squanders itself is the same extravagance as the elaborate and
contorted syllogisms of the logicians of the period. Virgil,
Racine, Poussin, are logical. Shakespeare also,—not to
mention Baudelaire. Chateaubriand is not.[1]

The architects of the Middle Ages did not restore "in the
style," like Viollet-le-Duc. If the choir of a Romanesque
church was destroyed by fire, they would rebuild it in
Gothic, without another thought. But consider in the
Cathedral at Le Mans the accord of the two, and the transition, the sudden leap, with such self-assurance, into splendour: there is living logic, like the logic of the orogeny of
the Alps or the anatomy of man.

2. The perfection of the virtue of art according to St.
Thomas consists in the act of judging [106]. As for manual

---

[1] Is this so very certain? I am afraid that Chateaubriand may have been
inserted merely to balance the sentence or because of an old prejudice not
entirely dissipated. I had better have said (it is the truth): Mallarmé, too,
is logical and Claudel is logical (and even terribly rational). And in a sphere
in which the rational has ceased to exist, from which the idea had been
deliberately ousted to make room for the architecture of dreams alone,
Pierre Reverdy is also logical, with a nocturnal unselfconscious logic incarnate in the spontaneity of feeling. Poetry such as Paul Éluard's obeys the
same law, " surrealist verses " too, when they have any poetic value. Even
chance is logical in the heart of a poet. (Is that any reason for being carried
away by it ? We should beware of taking for the normal conditions of poetry
experiments applied to reducing poetry to the impossible in order to test
its powers of resistance, and permitting only an ultimate germ to survive,
flickering upon the threshold of death.)

dexterity, it is a requisite condition, but extrinsic to art. It is even, though a necessity, a perpetual menace to art, inasmuch as it runs the risk of substituting the control of the muscular for the control of the intellectual *habit* and withdrawing the work from the influence of art. For there is an influence of art which, *per physicam et realem impressionem usque ad ipsam facultatem motivam membrorum*, proceeds from the mind, where art resides, to move the hand and make an artistic "formality" shine in the work [107]. A spiritual virtue can be so transmitted by a clumsy stroke.

Hence the charm to be found in the clumsiness of the Primitives. Clumsiness in itself is devoid of charm; it offers no attraction where poetry is lacking and becomes simply odious when it is, however little, deliberately contrived or parodied. But in the Primitives it was a sacred weakness revealing the subtle intellectuality of art [108].

Man lives so much *in sensibus*, finds it so difficult to keep on the level of the mind, that it may well be wondered if in art as in social life the development of material means and scientific technique, a good thing in itself, is not in reality an evil as far as the general average of art and civilisation is concerned. In this sphere, and beyond a certain limit, whatever removes an obstacle removes a source of strength, whatever removes a difficulty removes a glory.

When in an art gallery we leave the rooms of the Primitives for those which display the glories of oilpainting and a much more considerable material science, the foot advances over the floor but the soul sinks to the depths. It had been taking the air on the everlasting hills: it is now on the boards of a theatre—a magnificent theatre. In the sixteenth century deceit installed itself in painting, which began to like science for its own sake and to give the *illusion* of nature, to make us believe that in front of a picture we were in front of the landscape or the subject painted, not in front of a picture.

The great classics from Raphael to Greco, Claude Lorrain, and Watteau, succeeded in purifying art of such a lie: realism, and in a sense impressionism, acquiesced in it. Does cubism in our day, despite its tremendous deficiencies, represent the still stumbling screaming childhood of an art once more *pure*? The barbarous dogmatism of its theorists compels the strongest doubts and an apprehension that the new school may be endeavouring to set itself absolutely free from naturalist imitation only to become immovably fixed in *stultae quaestiones* [109], by denying the first conditions which essentially distinguish Painting from the other arts, from Poetry, for instance, or Logic.[1]

There is, however, to be observed in a few of the artists—painters, poets and musicians—whom Criticism lodged once upon a time at the Sign of the Cube (an astonishingly extensible cube) a most praiseworthy effort to attain the logical coherence, the simplicity and purity of means, which properly constitute the veracity of art. All *the best people*, nowadays, want the classical [109*b*]. I know nothing in contemporary production more sincerely *classical* than the music of Erik Satie: "Never the spell of the enchanter, never a refrain, never a suggestive caress, no fever or noxious emanation. Satie never 'stirs the pool'" [110]. It is the poetry of childhood composed by a master craftsman.

3. Cubism has rather vehemently stated the problem of *imitation* in art. Art, as such, consists not in imitating but in making, in composing or constructing, and that according to the laws of the very thing to be placed in being (ship, house, carpet, coloured canvas or hewn block of stone). This requisite of its generic concept preponderates over everything else in it: and to allot to it for essential end the representation of the real is to destroy it. Plato, with his theory of various degrees of imitation and poetry as an illusion [111], misconceives, like all extravagant intellectualists, the peculiar nature of art; hence his contempt for poetry: it is clear that if art were a means *of knowledge*, it would be wildly inferior to geometry [112].

---

[1] Or rather by denying the conditions which distinguish Painting from Art considered in its generic concept alone. The text was written more than ten years ago, and to-day the Cubist school has ceased to exist. But its consequences have not been lost; whatever the present state of theories may be, the Cubist reaction, by recalling painting to the essential requisites of art in general, did, in fact, render the very great service of recalling painting to itself.

But if art, as such, is far removed from imitation, the Fine Arts, as ordered to Beauty, are related to imitation, in a way difficult enough to define.

"*Imitation* is natural to mankind from childhood . . . , man is the most imitative of animals; through imitation he acquires his first knowledge and from imitations everyone derives pleasure. Works of art prove this, for the very things it gives us pain to see, we enjoy looking at in exact reproductions, the forms, for example, of the most horrible beasts, and corpses. The reason is that to be learning something is the pleasantest thing in the world not only to philosophers but to the rest of men . . ." [113]. When Aristotle wrote this with reference to the first causes of poetry, he was propounding a specific condition imposed upon the Fine Arts, a condition grasped in their earliest origin. But Aristotle is to be understood here in the most *formal* way. If the Philosopher, pursuing his usual method, goes straight to the primitive elementary case, it would be a complete mistake to stop there and to restrict the word "imitation" to its popularly accepted meaning of *exact reproduction or representation of a given reality*. When the man of the reindeer age scrawled the shapes of animals on the walls of caves he was no doubt principally moved by the pleasure of reproducing something exactly [114]. But the *joy of imitation* has since then become remarkably purified. I will try to sharpen the point of this idea of imitation in art.

The Fine Arts aim at producing, by the object they make, joy or delight in the mind through the intuition of the senses : the object of painting, said Poussin, is delight. Such joy is not the joy of the simple act of knowing, the joy of possessing knowledge, of having truth. It is a joy overflowing from such an act, when the object upon which it is brought to bear is well proportioned to the mind.

Such joy, therefore, presupposes knowledge, and the more knowledge there is, the more things given to the mind, the greater will be the possibility of joy. For this reason art, as ordered to beauty, never stops—at all events when its object permits it—at shapes or colours, or at sounds or words, considered in themselves and *as things* (they must

be so considered to begin with, that is the first condition),
but considers them *also* as making known something other
than themselves, that is to say *as symbols*. And the thing
symbolised can be in turn a symbol, and the more charged
with symbolism the work of art (but spontaneous symbolism
intuitively apprehended, not hieroglyphic symbolism), the
more immense, the richer and the higher will be the possibility of joy and beauty. The beauty of a picture or a statue
is thus incomparably richer than the beauty of a carpet, a
Venetian glass, or an amphora.

In this sense, Painting, Sculpture, Poetry, Music, even
Dancing, are imitative arts, that is to say arts realising the
beauty of the work and producing the joy of the soul by the
use of imitation or by producing through the medium of
certain sensible symbols the spontaneous presence in, the
mind of something over and above such symbols. Painting
imitates with colours and plane forms given things outside
us, Music *imitates* with sound and rhythms—and Dancing
with rhythm alone, "the character and temperament,"
in Aristotle's phrase [115], of the personages represented,
and the movements of the soul, the invisible world stirring
within us. Making allowances for such a difference in regard
to the object symbolised, Painting is no more imitative than
Music, and Music no less imitative than Painting if "imitation" be understood exactly in the sense just defined.

But the joy procured by the beautiful does not consist
formally in the act of knowing reality or in the act of conformity with what is; it does not depend upon the perfection
of the imitation as a reproduction of the real, or the fidelity
of the representation. Imitation as reproduction or representation of the real—in other words, imitation *materially
considered*—is merely a means, not an end; it relates, along
with manual dexterity, to the artistic activity, but no more
constitutes it. And the things made present to the soul
by the sensible symbols of art—by rhythm, sound, line,
colour, form, volume, words, metre, rhyme and image,
the *proximate matter* of art—are themselves merely a
material element of the beauty of the work, just like the
symbols in question; they are the *remote matter,* so to speak,
at the disposal of the artist, on which he must make the

brilliance of a form, the light of being, shine. To set up the perfection of imitation materially considered as an end would therefore involve ordering oneself with a view to what is purely material in the work of art; a servile imitation absolutely foreign to art [116].

What is required is not that the representation shall conform exactly to a given reality, but that through the material elements of the beauty of the work there shall be transmitted, sovereign and entire, the brilliance of a form[1]—of a form, and therefore of *some truth*; in that sense the great phrase of the Platonists, *splendor veri*, abides for ever. But if the joy produced by a work of beauty proceeds from *some truth*, it does not proceed from the truth of *imitation as a reproduction of things*, it proceeds from the perfection with which the work expresses or manifests form, in the metaphysical sense of the word [116b], it proceeds from the truth *of imitation as manifestation of a form*. There is the *formal element* of imitation in art, the expression or manifestation, in a suitably proportioned work, of some secret principle of intelligibility shining forth. There the *joy of imitation* in art is brought to bear. And it is that which gives art its *universal* value.

What constitutes the austerity of the truly classical is such a subordination of the matter to the light of the form so manifested as admits into the work no material element from things or the subject except what is absolutely necessary

---

[1] I have indicated in the note to page 28 in what sense this " brilliance of a form " is to be understood. It is not a question of the brilliance or facility with which the work evokes objects already known, ideas, feelings or *things*. The very things evoked, feelings, ideas and representations, are for the artist merely materials and means, still symbols. To stop to explain the power of poetry by the musicality of sounds would be to argue a very summary hedonism. A fine verse takes hold of the soul by spiritual corres- pondences, in themselves inexpressible, which are the special revelation of the right arrangement of words. " Obscurity " or " clarity " is then a matter of secondary importance.

Nor should it be forgotten that " the obscurity of a passage is the product of two factors : the thing read and the being who reads it. The latter rarely blames himself" (Paul VALÉRY, ap. Frédéric LEFÈVRE, *Entretiens*, Paris, 1926). Few great artists have escaped the reproach of obscurity from their contemporaries. Many minor artists, no doubt, make themselves obscure to compel admiration. At all events, if subjectivism *à la* Hamlet has more devotees to-day than when Max Jacob wrote his *Art Poétique*, modern poetry in its deepest tendency, far from searching for obscurity for its own sake, " rages," on the contrary, " at not being understood."

to support or transmit this light and would otherwise dull or "debauch" the eye, the ear or the mind [116c]. Compare from this point of view Gregorian plain-chant or the music of Bach with the music of Wagner or Stravinsky.[1]

Confronted with the work of beauty, as has already been said, the mind rejoices without discoursing. If art then manifests or expresses *in matter* a certain radiation of being, a certain form, a certain soul, a certain truth—"Oh ! you'll make a *clean breast of it* in the end," said Carrière to a sitter —it does not express it in the soul conceptually and discursively. It suggests without conveying absolute knowledge, and expresses what our ideas are impotent to signify. *A, a, a,* exclaims Jeremias, *Domine Deus, ecce nescio loqui* [117]. But song begins where speech breaks off, *exsultatio mentis prorumpens in vocem* [118].

In the case of the arts which appeal to the eye (painting and sculpture), or to the mind (poetry), a straighter necessity of imitation or symbolising is imposed upon the art from outside, because of the faculty in play. That faculty must rejoice, as a principal if it is the mind, secondarily and instrumentally if it is the sight [119]. Now sight and mind, being in the highest degree cognitive and directed to an object, cannot experience complete joy unless they have sufficiently lively knowledge of an object—in itself, no doubt also a symbol—symbolised to them by volume, colour or words. The eye and the mind then seek to perceive or recognise in the work something they can understand. And this is no doubt merely a condition extrinsic to the art itself considered formally,[2] an obscure poem may be better than a clear poem: nevertheless, poetic values being equal,

---

[1] I regret having thus spoken of Stravinsky. All I had heard was *Le Sacre du Printemps*, and I should have perceived then that Stravinsky was turning his back on everything we find distasteful in Wagner. Since then he has shown that genius conserves and increases its strength by renewing it in light. Exuberant with truth, his admirably disciplined work teaches the best lesson of any to-day of grandeur and creative energy, and best answers the strict classical " austerity " here in question. His purity, his authenticity, his glorious spiritual strength, are to the gigantism of Parsifal and the Tetralogy as a miracle of Moses to the enchantments of the Egyptians.

[2] A condition affecting what has been described above (cf. p. 58) as the remote matter of art.

the soul will derive greater enjoyment from the clear poem, and if the obscurity be too great, if the symbols cease to be symbols and become puzzles, the nature of our faculties will begin to expostulate. The artist is always to a certain extent doing violence to nature, and yet if he did not take account of this necessity, he would be offending, in a sort of idealist vertigo, the *material* or *subjective conditions* which art is humanly constrained to satisfy. Therein lies the danger of foolhardy voyages, however glorious in other respects, to the *Cape of Good Hope*, and of poetry which "teases eternity" by deliberately clouding the idea under films of images contrived with exquisite taste. When a cubist in a revolt against impressionism or naturism declares that a picture, like a cushion, should be as *beautiful* as ever when turned upside down, his assertion is a very interesting return (very instructive too, if properly understood) to the laws of absolute constructive coherence of *art* in general [120]; but he leaves out of account both the subjective conditions and the special requisites of what constitutes beauty in *painting*.

Nevertheless, if "imitation" were to be understood as meaning *exact reproduction or copy of reality* [121], it would have to be admitted that, apart from the art of the cartographer or the draughtsman of anatomical plates, there is no art of imitation. In that sense, and however deplorable his precepts may be in other respects, Gauguin, in maintaining that painters should give up *painting what they saw*, was formulating an elementary truth which the Masters have never ceased to practise. Cézanne's familiar dictum expressed the same truth: "What we must do is Poussin over again on nature. That's the whole secret" [123]. The imitative arts aim neither at copying the appearance of nature nor at depicting "the ideal," but at making something beautiful by the display of a *form* with the help of visible symbols.

The human artist or poet whose mind is not, like the Divine Mind, the cause of things, cannot draw this form complete out of his creative spirit: he goes and gathers it first and foremost in the vast treasure of created things, of sensitive nature as of the world of souls, and of the interior

world of his own soul. From this point of view he is first
and foremost a man who sees more deeply than other men
and discovers in reality spiritual radiations which others
are unable to discern [124]. But to make these radiations
shine out in his work and so to be truly docile and faithful
to the visible Spirit at play in things, he can, and indeed
he must to some extent, deform, reconstruct and trans-
figure the material appearance of nature. Even in a portrait
which is "a speaking likeness" of its subject—in Holbein's
drawings for example—it is always a form conceived in the
mind of the artist and truly brought to birth in that mind
which is expressed by the work, true portraits being merely
the "ideal reconstruction of individuals" [125].

Art, then, is fundamentally constructive and creative.
It is the faculty of producing, not of course *ex nihilo*, but
out of a pre-existing matter, a new creature, an original
being capable in its turn of moving a human soul. The new
creature is the fruit of a spiritual marriage uniting the activity
of the artist to the passivity of a given matter.

Hence the feeling in the artist of his special dignity. He
is as it were an associate of God in the making of works of
beauty; by developing the faculties with which the Creator
has endowed him—"for every perfect gift cometh from on
high and down from the Father of light"—and making
use of created matter, he creates as it were in the second
degree. *Operatio artis fundatur super operationem naturae,
et haec super creationem* [126].

Artistic creation does not copy God's creation, but
continues it. And even as the trace and image of God
appear in His creatures, so the human character is impressed
upon the work of art, the full, sensitive and spiritual character
not of the hands only but of the whole soul. Before the work
of art passes by a transitive action from art into matter, the
conception of art must itself have taken place within the
soul by an immanent and vital action, like the procession
of the mental word. *Processus artis est duplex, scilicet
artis a corde artificis, et artificiatorum ab arte* [127].

If the artist studies and cherishes nature as much as and
much more than the works of the masters, it is not to copy

nature, but to *base himself* upon nature, and because it is not enough for him to be a pupil of the masters: he must be God's pupil, for God knows the rules governing the making of works of beauty [128]. Nature concerns the artist essentially, simply because it is a derivation from the divine art in things, *ratio artis divinae indita rebus.* The artist, whether he knows it or not, is consulting God when he looks at things.

> *They exist but for a moment, but for all that they were fine!*
> *He were ignorant of his art who found the slightest flaw in*
> *Thine.* [129]

Nature is therefore in the first place a stimulus and a check to artists, not a model to be slavishly copied. Ask real painters how they need her. They stand before her in timidity and awe, but with the timidity of modesty, not of servility. They imitate her, in a truly *filial* spirit, and according to the creative agility of the spirit; but their imitation is not literal and servile. As we were coming back after a walk in winter time, Rouault told me that looking at the countryside under the snow in the sunshine he had realised how to paint the white trees of spring. "The model," said Renoir [130], "is there only to set me alight, to let me dare things I could never imagine without it . . . and it makes me come a cropper, if ever I go too far." Such freedom do the sons of the Creator enjoy.

4. Art has to be on its guard not only against being carried away by manual dexterity and servile imitation, but also against other foreign elements which threaten its purity. For example, the beauty to which it tends produces a delight, but the high delight of the spirit, the absolutely contrary of what is called pleasure, or the agreeable tickling of the sensibility; and if art seeks to *please*, it commits a betrayal and tells a lie So its *effect* is to produce emotion, but if it *aims* at emotion, at affecting or rousing the passions, it becomes adulterate, and another element of deceit thereby enters into it [131].

This is as true of music as of the other arts. Music no

doubt has this peculiarity that, symbolising by rhythm and sound the very movements of the soul—*cantare amantis est*—when it produces emotion, it produces precisely what it symbolises. But such production is not its object, any more than a representation or description of the emotions. The emotions which it evokes in the soul by sound and rhythm are the *matter* by which it ought to give us the experienced joy of a spiritual form, of a transcendent order, of the brilliance of being. So music, like tragedy, purifies the passions [132] by developing them within the limits and in the order of beauty, harmonising them with the intelligence, in a harmony which fallen nature experiences nowhere else.

The term *thesis* will be applied to any intention extrinsic to the work itself, when the thought inspired by such an intention does not act upon the work by means of the artistic habit moved instrumentally, but puts itself in juxtaposition to the habit so as itself to act directly upon the work. In such a case the work is not wholly produced by the artistic habit or wholly by the thought so inspired, but partly by one and partly by the other, like a boat pulled by two men. In this sense any thesis, whether it profess to demonstrate or to move, is an alien importation in art and as such an impurity. It imposes upon art, in its own sphere, that is to say in the actual production of the work, an alien rule and end; it prevents the work of art issuing from the heart of the artist with the spontaneity of a perfect fruit; it betrays calculation, a dualism between the intelligence of the artist and his sensibility, which the object of art is to have united.

I will willingly suffer the domination of the *object* which the artist has conceived and which he puts before my eyes; I will then yield myself unreservedly to the emotion roused in him and me by one same beauty, one same transcendental in which we communicate. But I refuse to suffer the domination of an art which deliberately contrives means of suggestion to seduce my subconsciousness, I resist an emotion which the will of a man claims to impose upon me. The artist ought to be as objective as the man of learning, in the sense that his only thought for the spectator should be to give him something beautiful, or *well-made*, as the only thought the man of learning has for his hearer is to deliver him the truth. The cathedral builders had no sort of thesis in mind. They were, in Dulac's fine phrase, "men unconscious of themselves" [133]. They did not want to demonstrate the propriety of Christian dogma or to suggest by some artifice a *Christian emotion*. They even thought very much less about making a work of beauty than turning out good work. They had the Faith, and as they were, so did they work. Their achievement revealed God's truth, but without *doing it on purpose*, and because it was not done on purpose.

VIII

CHRISTIAN ART

By Christian art I do not mean *ecclesiastical art*, an art specified by an object, an end, and definite rules, merely a particular, and notable, application of art. By Christian art I mean art bearing on the face of it the character of Christianity. Christian art in this sense is not a particular species of the genus art; we do not talk of Christian art as we do of pictorial or poetic, Gothic or Byzantine art. A young man does not say to himself "I am going in for Christian art," as he might say "I am going in for agriculture." There is no school for teaching Christian art [134]. The definition of Christian art is to be found in its subject and its spirit; we talk of Christian art or the art of a Christian as we talk of the art of the bee or the art of man. It is the art of humanity redeemed. It is implanted in the Christian soul, by the side of the running waters, under the sky of the theological virtues, amid the breaths of the seven gifts of the Spirit. It is natural for it to bear Christian fruit.

Everything, sacred and profane, belongs to it. It is at home in the whole range of man's industry and joy. Symphony or ballet, film or novel, landscape or still life, vaudeville or opera, it can be as apparent in them all as in the stained-glass windows and statues of churches.

But, it may be objected, is this Christian art not a myth? Can it so much as be conceived? Is art not pagan by birth and tied to sin—even as man is born a sinner? But grace heals the wounds of nature. Do not say that Christian art is impossible [134b]. Say rather that it is difficult, doubly difficult—difficulty squared, because it is difficult to be an artist and very difficult to be a Christian, and because the whole difficulty is not merely the sum but the product of these two difficulties multiplied by one another, for it is a question of reconciling two absolutes. Say that the difficulty becomes excruciating when the whole life of the age is far removed from Christ, for the artist is greatly dependent upon the spirit of the time. But has courage ever been lacking on the earth ?

Consider also that wherever art, Egyptian, Greek or Chinese, has attained a certain degree of grandeur and purity, it is already Christian, Christian in hope, because every spiritual splendour is a promise and a symbol of the divine harmonies of the Gospel.

Inspiration is not a mythological accessory only. There is a real inspiration, proceeding not from the Muses, but from the living God, a special impulse of the natural order [134c], whereby the first Mind gives the artist, when it pleases, a creative impulse transcending the limits of reason and employing as it elevates every rational energy of art. Man of his free will can obey or destroy such an impetus. This inspiration which descends from God, the author of nature, is as it were a symbol of supernatural inspiration. For an art to arise which shall be Christian not only in hope but in fact, truly freed by grace, both forms of inspiration will have to be united at its most secret source.

If you want to produce Christian work, be a Christian, and try to make a work of beauty into which you have put your heart; do not adopt a Christian pose.

Do not make the absurd attempt to sever in yourself the artist and the Christian. They are one, if you really *are* a Christian, and if your art is not isolated from your soul by some æsthetic system. But apply only the artist in you to the work in hand; precisely because they are one, the work will be as wholly of the one as of the other.

Do not *separate* your art from your faith. But leave *distinct* what is distinct. Do not try to blend by force what life unites so well. If you were to make your æsthetic an article of faith, you would spoil your faith. If you were to make your devotion a rule of artistic operation, or turn the desire to edify into a method of your art, you would spoil your art.

2. The whole soul of the artist affects and controls his work, but it should only affect and control it *by the artistic habit*. Art will suffer no division here. It will admit no foreign element to come jostling it, to interpose its own

system in the production of the work. Subdue it, and it will serve your will. Use violence, and no good will result. A Christian work would have the artist, as artist, free.

But it will be Christian, it will reveal in its beauty the interior reflection of the brilliance of grace, only on condition that it overflows from a heart possessed by grace. For the virtue of art which directly affects and controls it pre-supposes the rectification of the appetite so far as the beauty of the work is concerned. And if the beauty of the work is Christian, it is because the appetite of the artist is rectified in regard to such a beauty, and because Christ is present in the soul of the artist by love. The quality of the work in such a case is the effusion of the love from which it proceeds, which also moves the virtue of art like an instrument. So it is by reason of an intrinsic super-elevation that the art is Christian, and such super-elevation takes place through love.

The consequence is that the work will be Christian in proportion as the love is alive. Let there be no mistake: it is the actuality of love, contemplation in charity, which is here required. A Christian work would have the artist, as man, a saint.

It would have him possessed by love. Then he may go and do as he likes. Where the note struck by the work is less purely Christian, there has been some defect in the purity of the love [135]. *Art demands tranquillity*, said Fra Angelico, *and to paint the things of Christ, the artist must live with Christ.* It is the only remark of his which has been preserved, a mere fragment. . . .

It would be idle therefore to try to discover a technique, a style, a system of rules or a method of work peculiar to Christian art. An art germinating and developing amongst Christian men admits of an infinite variety. But all such forms of art will bear a family likeness and all differ sub-stantially from non-Christian forms of art, as the flora of the mountains differs from the flora of the plains. Consider the Liturgy, the transcendent, super-eminent type of Christian art-forms; the Spirit of God in Person fashioned it, for His own pleasure [136].

The Liturgy, however, is not absolutely unchangeable; it suffers the passage of time. In the Liturgy eternity renews its

c

youth. And the Maronite or Pravoslav liturgy is not the Roman liturgy; there are many mansions in Heaven. There is nothing more beautiful than a High Mass, a dance before the Ark in slow motion, more majestic than the advance of the hosts of Heaven. And yet the Church, in the Mass, is not searching for beauty or decorative motifs or a means of touching the heart. Her sole object is worship and union with her Saviour, and from this loving worship an excess of beauty overflows.

3. Beautiful things are rare. What exceptional conditions must be presupposed for a civilisation to unite, and in the same men, art and contemplation ! Under the burden of a nature for ever in revolt and for ever stumbling, Christianity has sprouted everywhere, in art and the world, but it has never succeeded, except in the Middle Ages and amid difficulties and deficiencies innumerable, in creating an art of its own, like a world of its own, and that is not surprising. Classical art has produced many Christian works, admirable of their kind. Nevertheless, can it be said that such a form of art considered in itself still retains the original flavour of the Christian climate ? It is a form born in a strange land, and transplanted.

If amid the indescribable catastrophes which the modern world invites there should occur a moment, however brief, of pure Christian springtime—a Palm Sunday for the Church, a short Hosanna from the distracted earth to the Son of David—the reflowering of a truly Christian art, the resurrection to active life of mind and spirit may then be reasonably expected for the joy of angels and men. There is already some indication of such an art in the individual efforts of a few artists during the last fifty years, some of whom are to be reckoned among the greatest. But we must above all be careful not to elicit or isolate it prematurely, by an academic effort, from the main movement of contemporary art [137]. It will emerge and impose itself only if it springs spontaneously from a common renewal of art and sanctity in the world.

4. Christianity does not make art *easy*. It deprives it of many facile means, it stops its progress in many directions,

but in order to raise its level. In the very creation of these salutary difficulties, it elevates art from within, brings to its knowledge a hidden beauty more delightful than light, gives it what the artist needs most, simplicity, the peace of reverent fear and love, such innocence as makes matter docile to men and fraternal.

IX

ART AND MORALITY

THE artistic habit is concerned only with the work to be done. It certainly makes allowance for the objective conditions (practical use, object intended, etc.) which the work must fulfil—a statue made to be prayed before is a different thing from a garden statue. But simply because the beauty of the work is itself involved in such considerations, a work ill adapted to such conditions lacks proportion and therefore beauty. The sole end of art is the work itself and its beauty.

But for the man working, the work to be done of itself comes into the line of morality [137b], and so is merely a means. If the artist were to take for the final end of his activity, that is to say for beatitude, the end of his art or the beauty of his work, he would be, purely and simply, an idolater [138]. It is therefore absolutely necessary for the artist, *qua* man, to work for something other than his work, something better beloved. God is infinitely more lovable than Art.

1. God is jealous. "The law of divine love knows no mercy," said Mélanie de la Salette. "Love truly sacrifices: it desires the death of everything not itself." Unhappy the artist whose heart is divided! The blessed Angelico would have abandoned his painting without a murmur to go and keep geese if obedience had required it of him. Therefore a creative stream gushed from his peaceful bosom. God left him that, because he had renounced it.

Art has no right against God. There is no good opposed to God or the ultimate Good of human life. Art in its own demesne is sovereign like wisdom; it is not subordinate by its object to wisdom or prudence or any other virtue. But by the subject and in the subject it is subordinate to the good of the subject; so far as it finds itself in man and is made use of by the freedom of man, it is subordinate to the end of man and the human virtues. Moreover, "if an art produces objects which men cannot use without committing sin, the artist producing such works himself commits sin, since he directly offers his neighbour the occasion to commit sin; as if one were to make idols for idolatry. As for the arts whose products can be put to a good or evil use, they are permissible; but nevertheless, if the products of some of them are put *in the majority of cases* to an evil use, they must, though permissible in themselves, be driven out of the State by the intervention of the Prince, *secundum documenta Platonis"* [139]. Fortunately for the rights of man, our fine States have no Prince, and the workers in the service of idolatry and lechery, of dressmaking or literature, are not troubled by Plato.

Because it is in man and because its good is not the good of man, art is subject in its exercise to a control from without, imposed in the name of a higher end, the very beatitude of the living creature in whom it resides. In the case of the Christian such control is unattended by any constraint, because the immanent order of charity makes it connatural to him and law has become his own interior inclination: *spiritualis homo non est sub lege.* To him may be said: *Ama, et fac quod vis*; if only you love, you may do as you please, you will never offend love. A work of art which is an offence to God offends him too, and, having nothing left wherewith to give delight, at once loses in his eyes all reason for being beautiful.

2. There is according to Aristotle [140] a double good in respect of a multitude—for instance, an army; one in the multitude itself, and such is discipline in the army, the other separate from the multitude, and such is the good of the Commander. And the latter is the better, because to it the other is subordinate, discipline in the army being intended to realise the good of the Commander, that is to say the will of the Commander in winning the victory [141]. The inference is that the contemplative, being ordered directly to the "separate common good" of the whole universe, that is to say to God, serves better than any other the common good of the human multitude; for the "intrinsic common good" of the multitude, the social common good,

depends upon the "separate common good," which is superior to it. The same will be the case, by analogy and when all allowance is made, with all those, metaphysicians or artists, whose activities border on the transcendental order, truth or beauty, and who have some share of wisdom, even only of natural wisdom. Leave the artist to his art: he serves the community better than the engineer or the tradesman.

This does not mean that he ought to ignore the State, either as a man (that is only too clear), or even as an artist. His problem is not to know if he should open his work to every human current flowing to his heart and in so doing pursue any particular human object; the individual case is the sole guide in such a matter, and prejudice would be unseemly. The sole problem for the artist is not to be a weakling: to be in possession of an art strong enough and direct enough to be always master of its subject without losing anything of its loftiness and purity; and in the very act of working to have in view the good of the work and that only, without being distracted or disturbed by the human ends pursued.

The truth is that art took to living its own separate life in the nineteenth century only because of the disheartening degradation of its surroundings; but its normal condition is altogether different. Æschylus, Dante and Cervantes did not write in glass-houses. On the other hand, there cannot in fact be any absolutely "gratuitous" work of art—except the universe. Not only is our act of artistic creation ordered to an ultimate end, true God or false god, but it must of necessity, because of its environment, be closely interested in certain proximate ends affecting the human order; the workman works for wages and the most disincarnate artist would like to influence souls and serve an idea, even if it be only an æsthetic idea. What is required is the perfect practical discrimination between the end pursued by the workman (*finis operantis*, said the Schoolmen) and the end to be served by the work (*finis operis*), so that the workman may work for his wages, but the work be controlled and set in being only in relation to its own proper good and nowise in relation to the wages earned; so that the artist may work for any and every human intention he likes, but the work taken by itself be performed and constructed for its own proper beauty alone.

It is the wildest of errors to think that the *ingenuousness* or the purity of a work of art depends upon a rupture with the principles which animate and move the human being, upon a line drawn between art and desire or love. It depends upon the *strength* of the principle generating the work or the *strength* of the artistic virtue.

There was a tree which said: "I will be tree and naught besides, and I will bear fruit which shall be pure fruit. Therefore I will not grow in earth which is not tree, or in a climate which is climate of Provence or of Vendée and not tree-climate. Shelter me from the air."

3. It would simplify many questions to make a distinction between art itself and its material or subjective conditions. Art being of man, why should it not depend upon the moods of the subject in which it is situate? They do not constitute it, but they determine its expression.

Art as such, for example, is *supra tempus* and *supra locum*, transcending, like the mind, every national boundary, and finding its limits only in the infinite fullness of beauty. Like science, philosophy and civilisation, by its very nature and object it is universal.

But it does not reside in an angelic mind: it is subject in a soul which is the substantial form of a living body and which, by the natural necessity in which it finds itself of learning and becoming perfect slowly and with difficulty, makes the animal it animates a naturally political animal. Art is therefore fundamentally dependent upon everything which the race and the State, spiritual tradition and history transmit to the body of man and his mind. By its subject and its roots, it belongs to a time and a country.

For this reason the most universal and most human works of art are those which bear most openly the mark of their country [142]. The century in which Pascal and Bossuet flourished was a century of robust nationalism. It was when France, at the time of the great peaceful victories of Cluny and in the reign of St. Louis, sent out over the whole of Christendom a most characteristically French—but Catholic in the first place—intellectual radiance that the world realised the purest and freest International of the spirit, and the most universal culture [143].

A robust *political and territorial* attachment to the nation is therefore the natural guardian of a proper genuine life and so of the very universality of the mind and of art: whereas a *metaphysical and religious* devotion to the nation, which would seek to make the mind the slave of the physiology of a race or the interests of a State, exposes art and every virtue of the spirit to the danger of death.

4. All our values depend upon the nature of our God.

Now God is Spirit. Progress—the word means, for every nature, tendency to its first principle [144]—is therefore a transition from the sensible to the rational and from the rational to the spiritual and from the less spiritual to the more spiritual. To civilise is to spiritualise.

Material progress can be of some help so far as it allows man leisure of soul. But if it be used merely to serve the will to dominate and to gratify a cupidity opening infinite jaws —*concupiscentia est infinita* [145]—it brings the world back to chaos at an accelerated speed. That is its way of tending to its first principle.

Art is a fundamental necessity in the human state. "No man," says St. Thomas following Aristotle, "can live without pleasure. Therefore a man deprived of the pleasures of the spirit goes over to the pleasures of the flesh" [146].

Art teaches men the pleasures of the spirit, and because it is itself sensitive and adapted to their nature, it is the better able to lead them to what is nobler than itself. So in natural life it plays the same part, so to speak, as the "sensible graces" in the spiritual life: and from afar off, without thinking, it prepares the human race for contemplation (the contemplation of the Saints) the spiritual joy of which surpasses every other joy [147] and seems to be the end of all human activities. For what useful purpose do servile work and trade serve, except to provide the body with the necessaries of life so that it may be in a state fit for contemplation ? What is the use of the moral virtues and prudence if not to procure that tranquillity of the passions and interior peace which contemplation needs ? To what end the whole government of civil life, if not to assure the exterior peace necessary to contemplation ? *"So that, properly considered, all the activities of human life seem to be for the service of those engaged in the contemplation of Truth"* [148].

If one were to attempt not an impossible classification of artists and works of art but to understand the normal hierarchy of the different types of art, it could only be done from this human point of view of their specific value in civilising or their degree of spirituality.

The scale would therefore descend from the beauty of Scripture and the Liturgy to the beauty of the mystic writers, and then to art in the proper sense of the term: the spiritual fullness of mediæval art, the rational harmony of Greek and classic art, the pathetic harmony of Shakespearean art. . . . The imaginative and verbal riches of romanticism, the instinct of the heart, for all its intimate lack of poise and spiritual penury, still keep alive within it the concept of art. With naturalism it disappears completely.

5. The magnificence of Julius II and Leo X embraced much more than a noble love of glory and beauty; with whatever concomitance of vanity, there passed over it a pure ray of the Spirit which has never failed the Church.

That great Contemplative, learned by the gift of Knowledge, has deep discernment of all the needs of the human heart: she knows the unique value of art. Therefore she has given it such powerful protection in the world. Ever so much more, she has summoned Art to the *opus Dei*, and asks Art to make perfumes of great price which she scatters on the head and feet of her Master. *Ut quid perditio ista?* murmur the philosophers. She continues to embalm the body of her Beloved, whose death she proclaims every day, *donec veniat*.

Do you think it possible that God, who "is called the Zealot," says Denys the Areopagite, "because He is consumed by love and zeal for everything that exists" [149], can contemptuously use artists and the fragile beauty which issues from their hands? Remember what He says of the men whom He has Himself appointed to sacred art: "Behold, the Lord hath called by name Beseleel, the son of Uri, the son of Hur, of the tribe of Juda, and hath filled him with the spirit of God, with wisdom and understanding and knowledge and all learning to devise and to work in gold and silver and brass, and in engraving stones, and in carpenters' work. Whatsoever can be devised artificially He hath given in his heart: Ooliab also, the son of Achisamech of the tribe of Dan: both of them hath he instructed with wisdom, to do carpenters' work, and tapestry, and embroidery in blue and in purple, and scarlet twice-dyed and fine linen, and to weave all things, and to invent all new things" [150].

6. The general opposition between Art and Prudence has already been indicated. This opposition becomes still more acute in the Fine Arts through the very transcendence of their object.

The Artist is subject in the sphere of his art to a kind of asceticism, which may require heroic sacrifices. He must be fundamentally in the direct line as regards the end of his art, for ever on his guard not only against the vulgar attractions of easy execution and success, but against a host of less subtle temptations, and against the slightest relaxation of his interior effort, for habits diminish, if unexercised [151], and ever so much more by any careless exercise not proportionate to their intensity [152]. The Artist must suffer sleepless nights, purify himself without ceasing, voluntarily abandon fertile places for barren places, full of insecurity. *In a certain sphere and from a particular point of view, in the sphere of making and from the point of view of the good of the work,* he must be humble and magnanimous, prudent, upright, strong, temperate, simple, pure, ingenuous. All these virtues which the Saints possess *simpliciter,* purely and simply, and in the line of the Sovereign Good, must inform the artist *secundum quid,* in a certain relation, in a line apart, extrahuman if not unhuman. So he easily assumes the tone of a moralist when speaking or writing about art, and he is well aware that he has a *virtue* to preserve. "We shelter an angel whom we never cease to offend. We ought to be the guardians of that angel. Shelter your virtue carefully . . ." [153].

But if such an analogy endows him with a singular nobility and explains the admiration he enjoys amongst men, it runs the risk of making him go pitiably astray, of making him lay up his treasure and set his heart upon an image of deceit, *ubi aerugo et tinea demolitur.*

The Prudent Man on the other hand, as such, judging all things from the angle of morality and in relation to the good of man, is absolutely ignorant of everything pertaining to art. He can no doubt, as he ought, judge the work of art as it affects morality [154]: he has no right to judge it as a work of art.

The work of art is the object of a singular conflict of virtues. Prudence, which considers it in its relation to morality, better deserves the name of virtue than Art [155], for, like every moral virtue, it makes the man who acts good purely and simply.

But Art is in itself a habit intrinsically nobler the closer it approximates to the speculative virtues, thereby acquiring more intellectual splendour; *simpliciter loquendo, illa virtus nobilior est, quae habet nobilius objectum.* Prudence is superior to Art in relation to man. In a pure and simple fashion Art—at any rate such art as, aiming at Beauty, is speculative in character—metaphysically is superior to Prudence [156].

What makes the conflict so bitter is the fact that Art is not subordinate to Prudence, as knowledge for instance is subordinate to wisdom, because of their objects. Nothing concerns Art but its objects; it has no concern whatever with subjects. Here is no definite line laid down as in the case of objective subordinations. Art and Prudence each claim dominion over every product of man's hands. From the point of view of poetic or, if you like, working values Prudence is not competent. From the point of view of human values and the position of the free act, to which everything with regard to the subject is subordinate, there is no limitation upon its rights to govern. To form a good judgement on the work both virtues are necessary.

In finding fault with a work of art, the Prudent Man, firmly established upon his moral virtue, has the certitude that he is defending against the Artist a sacred good, the good of Man, and he looks upon the Artist as a child or a madman. Perched on his intellectual habit, the Artist is certain of defending a good which is no less sacred, the good of Beauty, and looks as though he were crushing the Prudent Man under the weight of Aristotle's maxim: *Vita quae est secundum speculationem est melior quam quae secundum hominem* [157].

7. It is difficult therefore for the Prudent Man and the Artist to understand one another. The Contemplative and the Artist on the other hand, both perfected by an intellectual habit binding them to the transcendental order, are in a position to sympathise. They have also similar enemies. The Contemplative whose object is the *causa altissima* upon which everything else depends, knows the place and the value of art and understands the Artist. The Artist, as such, cannot judge the Contemplative but can guess his grandeur. If he really loves beauty and his heart is not besotted by some moral vice, as he goes past the Contemplative, he will recognise love and beauty.

Moreover, pursuing the line of his art, he tends without knowing it to pass beyond his art: as a plant unconsciously raises its stem to the sun, his eyes are turned, however low his habitation, towards subsisting Beauty, whose sweetness the Saints enjoy in a Radiance which Art and Reason cannot attain. "Painting and Sculpture," said Michelangelo in old age, "will lose their charm for the soul turned to that divine love which opened its arms upon the Cross to welcome us."

Consider Saint Catherine of Siena, that *apis argumentosa* who was the counsellor of a Pope and Princes of the Church, surrounded by artists and poets and leading them into Paradise. Perfectly prudent, but set far above Prudence, judging all things by Wisdom, which "in regard to all the intellectual virtues is architectonic," and in whose service

Prudence is "like a door-keeper in the service of the king" [158], the Saints are as free as the Spirit. The wise man, like God, is interested in the effort of every life.

"Delicate and not exclusive, he will yet be of our day: his heart, for all its contemplation, will yet know the works of men. . . ."

So Wisdom, being endowed with the outlook of God and ranging over Action and Making alike, alone can completely reconcile Art and Prudence.

Adam sinned, because he failed in contemplation: ever afterwards the heart of man was divided.

To turn away from Wisdom and contemplation and to aim lower than God is in a Christian civilisation the first cause of all disorder [159]. It is especially the cause of that ungodly divorce between Art and Prudence noticeable at times when Christian men have lost the strength to bear the burden of their riches. That is no doubt the reason why Prudence was sacrificed to Art at the time of the Italian Renaissance, in a civilisation solely inclined to the *virtu* of the Humanists, and why Art was sacrificed to Prudence in the nineteenth century, in "right thinking" circles inclined solely to Respectability.

THE FRONTIERS OF POETRY

Φεύγωμεν δὴ φίλην ἐς πατρίδα . . .
Πατρὶς δὴ ἡμῖν, ὅθενπερ ἤλθομεν,
Καὶ πατὴρ ἐκεῖ.

Plotinus: *Enneades*, 1, 8.

THIS Essay is not to be considered a work of *criticism*, either of literature or art. The author has too many principles in his head to make any such claim. He is only a philosopher. A philosopher's professional duty is to remain in the sky of metaphysics, the only enduring empyrean, from which he can perceive upside down the more or less stormy conflicts normally raging in the atmosphere of the plains, that is to say of particular realisations. *Art and Scholasticism*, far from fighting the battle of any particular school, has been well received in very different, even opposite, camps (opposed sometimes to the personal preferences of the author)—an indication that it is animated by a sufficiently philosophical, or universal, spirit. The study of first principles, in the practical as in the speculative order, is indeed the special province of philosophy: but a great gulf divides them from the work in which they find their ultimate application, a gulf which art alone can cross; and by very different paths, diverging ever more and more even when they are permissible, and they may in addition be only more or less successful [160].

If I had tried to make a synthesis of an historical and critical kind, I should have had to draw upon a far richer store of erudition. But for a philosophical work, erudition restricted to the essential, to the most accessible and significant examples, is sufficient [161].

This absolutely rigid separation once and for all well defined—it cannot be too strongly insisted upon—between the author's philosophic point of view and the point of view of artistic operation or criticism, it still remains to be observed, without displeasure, how easily in fact the very ancient principles recalled in the book rejoin the far-reaching purpose behind modern inquiries often considered to be fool-hardy. Such coincidences are instructive. The author has sometimes been reproached for his inclination to such researches, but he must confess that in the eight or nine years since this essay was written, it has only grown more profound. I would now like to aggravate my condition by embarking upon some explanations of certain tendencies in contemporary art. It is not a new chapter to be added to the others, which in my opinion are sufficient as they are. I desire merely to take up again in more concrete form some of the ideas more systematically exposed in the text (and also in the recent *Réponse à Jean Cocteau*), importing some fresh considerations based, to begin as a philosopher should, on the theory of divine ideas.

2. The ideas of God are not, like our concepts, representative symbols derived from things, intended to introduce into a created spirit the immensity of what has been achieved and of what is, and to make that spirit conform to existing things (actual or possible) independent of it. They precede things, creating them. Theologians therefore, to find some terrestrial analogy, compare them to the ideas of the artist.

Thomistic theology thereupon considers the peculiar nature of the idea of the artist and closely investigates what it implies. It is an idea of making or doing, a spiritual and immanent object contemplated in the mind, born of and nourished by the mind, living by the life of the mind, the immaterial matrix out of which the work is produced in being, an idea *formative* of things and not *formed* by them. Far from being measured by them like the speculative concept, it is the more independent of things the better it realises its peculiar essence: subduing them to its creative impregnation, it keeps them in such a state of subjection that to give the word "idea" its full force, with John of St. Thomas and his school, it must be said that we really have the idea of a thing only when we are capable of producing it [162]. It does not make the mind conform to reality but reality conform to the mind: for there is always resemblance, but in this case it is resemblance of a little matter to the abyss of the invisible engendering. In us the creative idea is not a pure intellectual form, because we are on the lowest rung of spirits: quite the contrary, the spiritual germ which impregnates our art, operating through sensitive organs and floundering in matter, is, so far as we are concerned, a mere atom of divinity hardly glimpsed, obscure to our own eyes, raising and irradiating the dough of sense and the elementary spontaneities. And above all this independence in regard to things, essential to art as such and the operative idea, is thwarted in our case by our condition—minds created in a body, placed in the world after creation, and compelled to draw first from created things the forms they use; in God alone does it appear perfectly. God sees in His Ideas every way in which His essence can be manifested and to their pattern He makes creatures, so setting the seal of His likeness over the whole range of creation, and detaching things from the life they had in Him and in which they were He, only to find again in them a vestige of Himself. Only here, on the high summits of Divinity, does the Idea as artisan-form obtain the complete fullness required of it by its notion.

Which is to say that art, like the mind (and art is simply the mind at work), considered separately and in its pure essence, realises all the perfection its nature postulates only by passing into pure Act. It is absurd, Aristotle observed, to attribute civil or political virtues to God. But in the sense in which the Gospel says: *Unus est bonus, Deus*, so we may say: *Unus est artifex, Deus.*

3. Here is a gleam of metaphysics thrown on the movement which impels—or only the other day impelled—our generation to search for *abstract music, abstract painting, abstract drama, abstract poetry* (I use the epithet in the sense in which it corresponds to the resolute effort undertaken in France since Mallarmé). To order contemporary art *to exist* as abstract art, discarding every condition determining its existence in the human subject, is to have it arrogate to itself the aseity of God. To require it *to tend* to abstract art like a curve to its asymptote [163], without rejecting the servitudes of its human estate, but ceaselessly

overcoming them, by straining its created bonds to the extreme limit of elasticity, is to require it to realise more fully its radical spirituality. Here is pride, there magnanimity, both aiming at the impossible, either of folly or of heroism. Blinding moment!—when the extremes of sin and virtue come close together and blend, each in that fusion proceeding to its destined place, the weak to the foolhardiness where it is destroyed, the strong to the virtue where it grows stronger.

To particularise: the whole discussion resolved itself into this, that art is faced by an antinomy (it is not alone in such a situation) between the supreme postulates of *its essential being* considered in itself and transcendentally, and the *conditions of existence* demanded by this same being as it is realised on this earth [164].

Where would the notion of "abstract art," driven to its furthest logical extremes, lead? To an art completely isolated from everything which was not its own peculiar rules of operation and the object to be created as such— in other words, separate and exempt from, and perfectly disinterested in regard to man and things. For art of itself— *recta ratio factibilium*—is not human like the moral virtues, and does not regulate itself by things like the speculative virtues; abstract it, and you have it absorbed in making being, regardless of beings. But then by dint of being itself it destroys itself, for its existence depends on man, in whom it subsists, and on things, which are its nourishment. The suicide of an angel—through forgetfulness of matter.

Remind it that "poetry is ontology" [165], that being *of man*, it can no more fence itself off from things than he; that being *in man*, art always ends by confessing in some way the weaknesses of man; and that in devouring the substance of the artist and the passions, the desires, the speculative and moral virtues which make it truly human, it is also devouring its own subject of inherence; that being in a way *for man*—if not in itself, at any rate so far as regards the use to which it is put [166]—it will in the end decay if it rejects either the constraints and limitations required from without by the good of man or the service of our common culture, which requires it to make itself intelligible, accessible, open, to shoulder the burden of the inheritance of reason and wisdom by which we live, "to interest the whole human race in its works and its refrain" [167]—and you remind it of the conditions of its existence, the sum of which is: humanity [168]. For all its irritation at the suggestion (an irritation excusable for the tone in which such remonstrances are generally addressed to it), it remains true nevertheless. A candid acceptance of these servitudes might, indeed, bring about a renewal of its own life, especially when a condition implicit in its own formal object is involved, as for instance regard for the *destination* of the work.

Nevertheless if art grows stronger in accepted servitudes, it is by fighting against them; and all the exigencies disclosed by its conditions of existence are, as we say, on the side of "subjective" and "material" causality. Art itself, we must not forget, is in a way an inhuman virtue, a straining after a gratuitously creative activity, entirely absorbed in its own mystery and its own laws of operation, refusing to subordinate itself either to the interests of man or to the evocation [169] of what already exists. In short, the straining towards abstract art follows from the very essence of art, once beauty has awakened it to self-consciousness. It cannot abandon it without treachery. A too flabby resignation to its conditions of existence is also suicide for art; the sin of materialism.

It will be noticed from this point of view that a return to religious practice, to an upright moral life or sound philosophy, does not of itself in the least import a concomitant recovery of art in its own line, but merely brings it back to normal conditions of existence—and the normal obligations these imply. This may reinvigorate its vitality and free it from all kinds of hindrances and obstacles (*removere prohibentia*), but it also makes it lose in æsthetic quality, for that is a mere question of dispositive causality, and all depends upon what advantage a sufficiently robust virtue of art will be able to derive from it.

Such is the profound conflict which art cannot escape. The solution is no doubt clear to the philosopher. Art must acquire that ideal independence, the desire for which is engraved upon its nature, in regard to the material obligations involved in its conditions of existence; it must turn these obligations to account, master them, show itself strong enough to shoulder them without stooping; it must not refuse them—that would be an admission of weakness.

But practically, for the artist, the solution is not so easy. There will in fact be a give and take. It will be necessary to aim too high; and precisely the better to dominate matter and be sure of fresh grips upon it the artist will appear to repudiate it, concealing a fresh energy behind such weakness. Mallarmé never intended to reduce the significance of words to nothing; he was preparing on the contrary a fresh way of approaching it.

At all events, however useful the resistance of the critical reason and the human environment may be, it is not through them, but by the impulse of invention itself, pursuing its course, that the necessary adjustments are made. Art rights itself by advancing further, not by stopping. The springs of the conditions of existence recoil spontaneously. Or it comes to be perceived that a too abstract effort was itself going astray and injuring a specific requirement of human art. In the ever-changing, never stationary, life which poets carry on through the whole length of time, Mallarmé and, in another order, Rimbaud one fine day become the past [170]. At that moment there appears in them something which is a stop, an end and not a beginning, an exhaustion of energy, against which a definition will have to be made. A fresh start will then ensue with a closer grasp of truth.

To bring this digression to an end, let it be added that those who advance along the path of tradition, *in via disciplinœ*, very naturally prefer to cling to what in art is attached to its conditions of existence; those who advance along the path of invention, *in via inventionis*, to what is attached to its abstract form or essence. So this distinction between essence and conditions of existence might possibly, if acknowledged, make its contribution to the formation of an equitable judgement on

That long quarrel between tradition and invention,
Between Order and Adventure,

mentioned by Apollinaire.

4. The problem of imitation, which, if only imitation be properly understood, concerns the formal element of art, is closely related to the questions just raised. The theological consideration of the working idea clearly shows how foreign to art is the servile imitation of the appearance of nature, for art's most fundamental demand is that the work make apparent not something else already made, but the spirit from which it proceeds. As God makes created participations of His being exist outside Himself, so the artist puts himself—not what he sees, but what he is—into what he makes. So anyone contemplating the myriad landscapes bearing God's signature at every revolution of light, or the features of any beast or man whatever, clearly sees that they are literally *inimitable* and that there is more humility in continuing in our own way the creative impulse than in striving to obtain a like effect in a picture.

The truth is, and it is the core of the mystery, that we have nothing but what we have received.

There is considerable truth in Wilde's paradoxes on lying; truth which, needless to say, has nothing to do with the shoddy Hegelianism with which he tricks it out. It is quite true that things are better in the mind than in themselves [171], that they acquire their full stature only when they have been expressed, and that they themselves pray to be assumed into the heaven of metaphysical or poetical thought, where they proceed to live outside time with a life which is universal. What would have become of the Trojan War without Homer? Unfortunate are the adventures which are never narrated.

But what Wilde, choked by the paper roses of his æstheticism, failed to understand is that our art does not derive from itself alone what it imparts to things; it spreads over them a secret which it first discovered in them, in their invisible substance or in their endless exchanges and correspondences. Take it out of "that blessed reality given once for all, in the centre of which we are situated" [172], and it ceases to be. It transforms, removes, brings closer together, transfigures; it does not create. It is by the way in which he changes the shape of the universe passing through his mind, in order to make a form apprehended in things shine upon a matter, that the artist impresses his signature upon his work. He recomposes for each, *according as the poetry in him changes him,* a world more real than the reality offered to the senses.

So, because it is subjected in the mind of a man the law of imitation, of resemblance, remains constant for our art but in a sense purified. It must transpose the secret rules of being in the manner of producing the work, and it must be as faithful and exact, in transforming reality according to the laws governing the work to be done, as science in conforming thereto. What it makes must resemble not the material appearance of things, but some one of the hidden significances whose iris God alone sees glittering on the neck of His creatures—and for that very reason it will also resemble the created mind which in its own way discerned those invisible colours. Resemblance, but a *spiritual* resemblance. Realism, if you like, but transcendental realism.

5. Such divination of the spiritual in the things of sense, which also will express itself in the things of sense, is what we properly call POETRY. Metaphysics also pursues the spiritual, but in a very different way, and with a very different formal object. Whereas it keeps to the line of *knowledge* and the contemplation of truth, poetry keeps to the line of *making* and the delight procured by beauty. The difference is capital and not to be overlooked without prejudice. One snatches at the spiritual in an idea, by the most abstract intellection; the other glimpses it in the flesh, by the point of the sense sharpened by the mind. One enjoys its possession only in the secluded retreat of the eternal regions; the other finds it at every cross-roads where the singular and the contingent meet. Both seek a super-reality, which one attains in the nature of things, and the other is content to touch in any symbol whatsoever. Metaphysics pursues essences and definitions, poetry every form glittering by the way, every reflection of an invisible order. The one isolates mystery in order to know it, the other, through the harmonies it constructs, handles and makes use of mystery like an unknown force.

Poetry in this sense—need it be observed?—is quite

the opposite of LITERATURE, in the sense (it was already so understood in the time of Verlaine) of a sort of deformation of which men of letters are the chosen victims—the sophistry of art, as difficult to rout as the ancient sophistry detested by Plato, and including all faked reproductions of beauty which make the work tell a lie every time the artist prefers himself to the work. Such an impurity in our art is the wound inflicted by original sin, and art never ceases to moan for it. For it is not itself a lie, as is commonly believed, on the pretext that its truth is not the truth of knowledge. It expresses the personality of the artist to the outside world in so far as the artist forgets his personality in his object [173], and in the (interior or exterior) reality which he displays transforming it. Literature puts the grin of personality upon the work. It would fain decorate God.

Literature is to art what vanity is to the moral life. Poetry, I have said elsewhere, is to one what grace is to the other.

Poetry in this sense is clearly not the privilege of poets. It forces every lock, lies in wait for you where you least expected it. You can receive the little shock by which it makes its presence known, which makes the distance still recede and unrolls the horizon of the heart, as much when looking at any common thing, a paste-board model, "silly pictures, door-mantels, stage decorations, back-cloths in the booths of a fair, sign-boards" [174], as when contemplating a masterpiece.

You read prospectuses and catalogues and the placards shouting aloud:
Here's your poetry this morning. . . .

The *Fine Arts*, however, and the art of the poet itself, being ordered to a transcendental world, are specially designed by nature to bring it into our midst. Their desire is to seize it [175]. When they meet poetry, each attains the principle of its own spirituality.

6. I have said that contemporary art, in tending to become "abstract," while running the risk of suicide because of the inhuman conditions in which it becomes involved, tends to

approximate to its first principle and to acquire a higher consciousness of its spirituality. It is inevitable that it should at the same time become more conscious of its relation to poetry, that it should clamour with a stronger desire and more despairingly for that thing, whatever it be, from which the best of its spiritual life proceeds. The search for the absolute purity of art will so at the same time be the search for the abstract substance of poetry. This, alas! is not a case of looking and finding.

Modern art is doing penance, wearing itself out, mortifying and scourging itself like an ascetic bent on self-destruction in order to obtain the grace of the Holy Ghost, and often remaining empty of what superabounds in a child. Rimbaud holds his peace. What was there in the heart of Rimbaud but that hunger for the poetic absolute [176], the pure spirit of poetry which bloweth where it listeth, without any man knowing whence it cometh or whither it goeth ? With the mysticism of light and darkness by which poetry symbolises with the supernatural without penetrating it, mimics it while proclaiming it, grace can blend its notes; but of itself it still remains far, far removed from the mysticism of the Saints, and is as available in Heaven as in Hell.

The capital importance of the parts played by Baudelaire and Rimbaud lies in the fact that they made modern art pass the frontiers of the spirit. But those are the regions of direst peril, there the weightiest metaphysical problems fall upon poetry, there the battle is waged between the good and the bad angels, and the bad angels are disguised as messengers of light.

7. Art opened its eyes upon itself at the time of the Renaissance. It may be said that in the past half-century it has been seized by another fit of introspection, provoking a revolution no less important. Work such as Picasso's shows a fearful progress in self-consciousness on the part of painting. Its lesson is as instructive for the philosopher as for the artist, and a philosopher may therefore be permitted a few words in which to express his point of view.

We can see Picasso spending an heroic will, courageously confronting the unknown to find a pure form of expression, free from even such human interferences and *literature* as proceed from the pride of the eyes and their acquired knowledge; hereafter painting will have made a step forward in its own peculiar mystery. At every moment he is close to committing the sin of the angels: any other would at such a height. I sometimes think that by dint of reducing painting to itself alone and its pure formal laws, he feels it giving way under his hand; he then bursts into a paroxysm of rage, lays hold of anything and nails it against a wall—always with an infallible sensibility—but he always saves himself, because in everything he touches he evokes an incomparable poetic substance.

Picasso comes up against poetry because he is a pure painter; there he is in line with the Masters, and recalls one of their most instructive lessons. Cocteau has rightly pointed out [177] that his paintings do not despise reality, they *are like* with that spiritual likeness—a "surreal" likeness, to use a word very true in itself—which I have already mentioned. There are times when one hesitates to decide whether it is inspired by a devil or a good angel. But not only are things transfigured in passing from his eye into his hand; another mystery can be guessed at the same time—the painter's soul and body struggling to take the place of his models, to drive away their substance, to come in and offer themselves under the appearances of the trifles portrayed in a picture, living on the canvas with a life which is not their own.

So the spiritual virtue of human art, once it has attained a certain altitude in its own heaven, perceives itself to be translating by analogies and symbols the movement of a superior, unattainable sphere. Rimbaud blasphemed at his inability to allay that kind of eucharistic passion which he had discovered in the heart of poetry. We cannot tell, for our understanding of the spiritual is imperfect, to what depths—at times in the reversed symbols of sin—art pursues its analogy with the supernatural. At a certain level of abandonment and anguish, it awakens impossible desires, and the poor human soul, which trusted it, is thrown on a nameless world, as close to, as far away from, truth as the reflection of your face in the deep water over which you lean. God alone, whom it desires without knowing, will thenceforth be able to content it; it has found what it was looking for, the strength of a surface by which to cross, but it needs the help of Omnipotence to take such a step.

8. Poetry (like metaphysics) is spiritual nourishment, but the savour of it is created and insufficient. There is only one eternal nourishment. Unhappy you who think yourselves ambitious, if you whet your appetites for anything less than the three divine Persons and the humanity of Christ.

It is a deadly error to expect poetry to provide the super-substantial nourishment of man.

The quest of the absolute, of perfect spiritual liberty, combined with the lack of any metaphysical and religious certitude, has caused many of our contemporaries, after Rimbaud, to fall into this error. In the midst of a despair whose occasionally tragic reality ought not to be overlooked, they expect from poetry alone an improbable solution of the problem of their lives, the possibility of an escape towards the super-human. And yet, Rimbaud had said it, *Charity is such a key*. Despite this luminous phrase, he remains the great personification of the error mentioned.

Let us follow our scholastic custom and proceed by exact definitions. We have seen that there are three terms to be distinguished: *poetry*, *art*, and "*literature*." I say that in the extreme Rimbaud's error consists on the one hand in confusing the latter two, in denouncing as "literature" art properly so-called,[1] on the other hand in separating the first two terms, and forcibly transferring poetry from the line of art to the line of morality, which leads to the exact opposite of Wilde's error: Wilde made life a means of

---

[1] Art begins with the mind and the will to select. The spontaneous welling up of images, without which there can be no poetry, *precedes and nourishes* the activity of the poet: and doubtless it is never the result of premeditation and calculation: this must be emphasised. As a general rule, however, the mind not only regulates but invites such an activity and gives it a direction. It then waits for the results, stops them as they issue, makes a selection and forms a judgement.

poetry: now poetry is being made the means of life (and death).

What is the result? We shall see men gifted with the sense of poetry load poetry with burdens against which its nature rebels, *onera importabilia*; we shall see them insist upon a picture, a piece of sculpture, or a poem, making "our abstract knowledge properly so called take a step forward" [178], opening the heart to a metaphysic, revealing to us sanctity. But poetry can only do that by cheating, and once more we are faced with a mirage; we are intimidated, and our eyes blinded by the irruption of exotic splendours. The most strenuous effort to get free from any kind of literature will so end by sheer force of circumstances in literature once more. Once this is perceived, there will be a ravaging of self. And a fresh deception will follow.

As for the sphere of action and human destiny, what element can poetry as regulating moral and spiritual life, poetry to *be realised in conduct*, introduce that is not counterfeit? Counterfeit of the supernatural and the miraculous, of grace and the heroic virtues. Disguised as an angel of counsel it will lead the human soul astray on false mystic ways [179]; and its spirituality, perverted from its meaning and diverted from its true place, under the appearance of a wholly profane interior conflict will give a new development to the old heresies of the free spirit. Purity! There can be no purity where the flesh is not crucified, or freedom where there is no love. Man is called to supernatural contemplation: to invite him to another darkness is to rob him of his possession. A revolution which does not effect a change of heart is a mere turning over of whitened sepulchres.

9. Poetry is the heaven of the working reason. To put forward the misdeeds of the spirit Poetry when it has gone astray as a pretext for refusing to acknowledge its rights in the line of art, to claim to bring art back to mere technique or amusement or pleasure, would be an unpardonable mistake, and useless too. It may be that a reaction like "Now don't let's budge a step from nature" may take place some day, and I am told that in Italy there are already signs of it, at any rate as regards painting. Nothing could be more

in harmony with the trend of fashion. If, supposing it really comes, such a reaction fails to integrate the spiritual values of contemporary inquiries (as the classical reaction, in France, did *not* fail to assimilate, at any rate in part, the spirit of Ronsard), it will only be an accident of no importance. Man is always severely punished for forgetting the metaphysical transcendence of poetry and that if in the work of creation the Word has been art, the Spirit has been poetry. "Because Poetry, oh my God! is You" [180].

There were times when art worked in a blessed innocence, in the conviction that it was only a trade, intended for the service or the amusement of mankind, and considering its function to be the painting of grapes to cheat birds, the celebration of feats of arms, the adornment of council chambers, the charming away of melancholy, the teaching and improving of the common people. It lived then in a state of bondage; which does not mean that it was enslaved. It did not deny its nature; it was unaware of itself. Thanks to an admirable misunderstanding, its native nobility and liberty, not proclaimed in ideas and words, in anything said, were respected in the silence of what is done: protected by its very obligations and its own humility. Poetry came to visit it in secret; never was it happier, never more productive.

Such times are gone and far gone; art cannot return to ignorance of itself and abandon all that consciousness has won for it. If it succeeds in finding a new spiritual equilibrium, it will be, on the contrary—in this I think that Valéry agrees with me—by *still greater* self-knowledge.

A parenthesis: there are many references in *Art and Scholasticism* to the Middle Ages. They are legitimate, because the Middle Ages are relatively the most *spiritual* period to be found in history and offer us an example very nearly realised—I do not deny the vices and defects—of principles which the author believes to be true. But time is irreversible and the example will serve best as an *analogy*. The same principles have to be realised to-day, but in an entirely new manner which it is very difficult to foresee (for there are countless possible historic realisations, as different as you like, of the same abstract principle). If as a result of our natural inclination to materialise everything, the spiritual analogy sank to be a mere material copy, in imitation of the fashions, in themselves particular, of historical realisation, it would be the danger of the Middle Ages which would have to be denounced. Much as I admire Romanesque and Gothic architecture, I remember the delight I felt in St. Peter's at Rome when I saw that Catholicism is not bound even to what I hold dearest. In that great light of reason most suitable to a religion publicly revealed, even Bernini was of service in testifying to the universality of my faith.

As for the Renaissance, the author's attitude with regard to it has not infrequently been misunderstood. There is in it a sort of "intentional virtue" directed to the worship of man, which has become the form of the modern world. But it is in the most immaterial order, whither metaphysics and theology alone penetrate, that it is to be discerned, without overlooking on that account all the normal developments taking their course elsewhere and affected *at first* only in their pure spiritual signification by the accident occurring in the high places. To observe that there came a moment when beauty, still retaining the fragrance of the virtues and prayer, began to fall away from its vows, to find pleasure in the picture of earthly love and youthful sensuality, is not to calumniate Florence. To remark that the spiritual curve of culture shows a decline ever since the Renaissance is not to express the wish that the Renaissance be deleted from human history. There is a parallelogram of forces. There is in the course of events a divine line to which our infidelity adds a component of deviation of varying intensity, but which Providence does not therefore abandon. If Erasmus and his friends had proportioned their means to the end they had in view and realised that to be right mere reason is not sufficient, above all if there had not been for so long such an abuse of grace in Christendom, the Renaissance would not have deviated so far from that line, humanism would not so soon have proved inhuman. There is nevertheless a lesson to be learned from God's patience: not to reap, even in desire, harvests sown with cockle.

Every strong civilisation imposes exterior constraints

upon art, because it subjects the whole domain of practice to the primacy of the good of man and powerfully orders all things to that good. Enough has been said of the advantages which art, if it chooses, can derive from such constraints. And not art only. The pitiable state of the modern world, a mere corpse of the Christian world, creates a specially ardent desire for the reinvention of a true civilisation. If such a desire were to remain unfulfilled and the universal dissolution to take its course, we should still find consolation, because as the world breaks up we see the things of the spirit gather together in places in the world but not of the world. Art and poetry are among them, and metaphysics and wisdom; the charity of the Saints will lead the choir. None of them has any permanent dwelling here below; each lives in casual shelters, waiting for the storm to pass. If the Spirit which floated over the waters must now hover above the ruins, what does it matter? It is sufficient if it comes. What is certain, at all events, is that we are approaching a time in which any hope set below the heart of Christ is doomed to disappointment.

10. Max Jacob thinks that the poetic activity which is taking place under the eyes of our contemporaries, and of which they are scarcely aware, is preparing the way for a revival of art as important as the advent of Cimabue and Giotto. Such a spring may, indeed, be at hand. Our Lord exhorts us to pay attention to the budding of the fig-trees which proclaims that summer is nigh. Great things foretell nothing; it is the little things which foretell the great.

Art, formally considered, seeks only to develop in history its internal logic, in complete disregard of our human interest. In fact, however, the occasional triumph of any one of the virtualities struggling within it results for the most part from the material causality or the dispositions of the subject. At the present day it is carried so far forward into the regions of the spirit, deeply involved in such cruelly metaphysical problems, that it cannot escape a choice of a religious kind. The search for abstract art, as attempted by the symbolists with such high hopes, is now, as regards art, utterly out of date; its orientation is towards Christ or Antichrist,[1] towards sheer destruction or faith. Is not every desire that exists torn between these two ways, and going forward divided, a prey to the absolute?

I do not forget that by the very nature of things one way is broader than the other and more comfortable. Evil is essentially easy. Because good is an integrity, whereas evil is a *deficiency*, and because evil does not act of itself but through good, whose parasite it is, it needs only a little good to be very successful in evil, whereas it requires a great deal of good to be slightly successful in good. There must be privileged epochs, and a State such as ours no longer is, for the art of a period to find its greatest chances in the line of good. Nor do I forget that extreme anguish makes what God requires more manifest and the succour of the superior virtues more necessary.

That in many cases at the present day art should elect for the devil is not surprising. But on the other hand anyone can see that in a small and not contemptible group it elects for Christ. Such an impetus will not be easy to stop. From this point of view the historical importance of Léon Bloy and Paul Claudel is incalculable. Through them the absolute of the Gospel has entered into the very sap of contemporary art. Formerly, in the great periods, religion preserved its dignity, which ordinary social life in the human State would gladly compromise into a mere means of amusing or, as Gide says, *flattering* an aristocracy [181]. Now that it is no longer recognised by public life, it must perform a like task in the secret and more profound sphere of intellectual life. It alone can help contemporary art to keep the best of its promises, I do not say by clothing it with a gaudy devotion, or in applying it directly to some work of evangelisation, but by enabling it to respect its own nature and take its true place. For only in the light of theology can it

---

[1] The unconcealed and palpable influence of the devil on an important part of contemporary literature is one of the significant phenomena of the history of our time. Léon Bloy imagined a moment when " the true Beelzebub " would make his entrance and, parodying Hugo, declare " in a voice arguing lordship of the abyss " : *Gentlemen, you are every one of you possessed.* It is at all events time to call the attention of exorcists to cases of *demoniac possession in literature,* a horribly grimacing species of the type.

completely acquire self-knowledge and recover from the false systems of metaphysics which obsess it. By showing us where moral truth and the genuine supernatural are situate, religion saves poetry from the absurdity of believing itself destined to transform ethics and life: saves it from overweening arrogance. But by teaching man to discern immaterial realities and the savour of the spirit, by linking poetry and art itself to God, it protects them against cowardice and self-abandonment, allows them to attain a more exalted and more rigorous idea of their essential spirituality, and to concentrate their inventive activity on the fine point thereof.

A deliverance of the values of contemporary art is therefore conceivable—it began half a century ago—a renaissance, which the analogy between the operative virtues and the virtues regulating the moral life would justify calling Christian, not in the specifically religious order only, but in the order of artistic creation itself.

Prudence and justice, fortitude and temperance: we should, to begin with, find the cardinal virtues there transposed into the order of the *factibile*, as characteristics of the work done, for they are by analogy the archetypes of the rules of every work of art. But such an art, already inspiring many works we admire, would bear the imprint of far different correspondences. It would in its way follow the lesson of the Gospel. It would know the meaning, for a fruit produced in the secrecy of the soul, of humility and poverty, spiritual chastity, obedience, high regard for the works of the Father, miracles worked in private, the concealment of good because of the eyes of men, the passage of light in our midst and its own received it not. It would understand with St. Thomas that understanding is the sister of mystery: and that it is as foolish to reject mystery because *Nonsense is not my strong point* as to reject understanding because one has a weakness for it. It would become fast friends with the wisdom of the Saints, would know the value of purity of heart, would learn how love and the seven gifts of the Spirit impose upon the works of man a more exalted rule than the rule of reason. Chaste fear, piety, strength, counsel, knowledge, intelligence, wisdom, "what would one say of a work bearing the visible traces of such gifts ?" [182].

We should then see complete harmony without waste or wavering between submission to the conditions of our human state, on which the virtues operative in the subject depend for their very existence, and the movement towards abstract art, which follows from the very essence of these virtues once they touch beauty—as in the Saints we see the harmony of a modest and cheerful submission to the necessities of human nature and an audacious movement towards pure spirit. The true equilibrium between the various mental energies associated in the production of the work would also be recognised. For if it is true that the direct practical reason is the formal element of art, the element, consequently, on which the Schoolmen owed it to themselves to insist most (confirmed in so doing by the testimony of the artists themselves, of a Delacroix no less than a Poussin), it is equally true that without the dynamism of the imagination, and the whole immense night of the animate body, this formal principle would be as little sufficient to art as a mortal soul is sufficient to itself without matter. And truly this enormous power of the senses is the more visible. Aristotle told us long ago that the νοῦς is nothing compared with the mass: it is the νοῦς nevertheless which is the more important.

But if the active point of the soul—the spiritual instinct in contact with the heaven of the transcendentals—on which poetry peculiarly depends is not moved in us by some special impulse proceeding from the first Intelligence, reason will play only a poor part, and, in its inability to penetrate the depths either from above or below, will prefer not to recognise them. Instead of the dialogue between the soul and the spirit—*spiritus vis animae*—it will be the conflict between the soul and the lower reason [183]. However true the observations of Poe and Baudelaire, Wilde and Valéry on the creative importance of the critical spirit may be, the estimate still fails to take account of the most divine; the spirit in us is placed between an obscurity which is superior by excess of transparency and an obscurity which is inferior by excess of opacity. The soul no doubt receives more fully than the spirit the rays from these two nights, but it is for Adam to judge all the voices which Eve hears. What some vainly look for on the extreme confines of sleep and abandonment to unconsciousness will be found on the extreme confines of watchfulness: watchfulness of the spirit, so subtle and so alert—prepared by interior silence— that it will detect on the edge of the shadow every shape passing beneath the starry vault of the heart. *Vigilate et orate:* here too the precept comes from the Gospel.

11. Will this new epoch flourish only in our desires? The elders have done and are doing their task, which is considerable; everything now depends upon a few young men in their twenties,—and, alas ! on the general conditions of human life, too, for every artistic period is a function of the whole civilisation. What is certain is that an art subject to the law of grace is such a difficult thing, requires such rare equilibria, that man, even Christian man, and as accomplished a poet as you like, is by himself incapable of it. The Spirit of God is essential.

We are so stupid, St. Thomas approximately teaches, that even provided with the infused virtues, theological and moral, we should certainly miss our salvation if the gifts of that Spirit did not come to the rescue of the feeble government of our reason. Art taken by itself has no need of such assistance; but the art I mean here, an art truly bearing the traces of the seven gifts, ought to proceed from a heart itself stirred by them. Let there be no mistake: by its height and the surmounting of obstacles it presupposes, such art would require souls in absolute submission to God. That does not make things easy.

12. "There is only one sorrow, the sorrow of not being a saint" [184]. The task is beyond our powers. It is when we are weakest that it is hardest of all,—could any weakness be greater than the weakness of our contemporaries ? A weak and unfortunate generation is once more bearing the burden of the future. Must we then give up the struggle ?

Consider, says Our Lord, serious people who undertake affairs of state. Which of you, wishing to build a tower, does not first sit down and calculate the expense and see if he will be able to reach the end of the work, for fear that when

D

he has laid the foundations and become unable to complete the building all who see it will mock him, saying "Behold a man who began to build but was unable to complete"? And what king about to make war on another king does not first sit down and reckon whether with ten thousand men he will be able to resist an aggressor coming to attack him with twenty thousand?

Which means to say: before setting to work for God and to fight against the devil, first calculate your forces; and if you consider yourself well enough equipped to begin, you are a fool, because the tower to be built costs an *outrageous price*, and the enemy coming out to meet you is an angel, before whom you are of no account. Realise that you are summoned to a task far beyond your strength. Get to know yourself so well that you cannot contemplate yourself without flinching. Then there will be room for hope. In the sure knowledge that you are "obliged to do the impossible" and that you can do the impossible in Him who strengthens you, then you are ready for a task which can be performed only through the Cross.

I am well aware that many people understand this parable differently. They fear God but are more afraid of the hosts of Satan, and in the end, after mature deliberation, conclude an agreement with the enemy, sending him from afar the delegation of their fears. The safest course is to leave him the difficult positions, poetry and philosophy, and to abandon to him intelligence. They are true Davids, advancing after every danger has been removed.

Others say and, in my view, with greater wisdom: we know that it is a fearful thing to bear the name of Christ before men, and what a paradox a Christian art must realise; what dangers attend the meeting between religion and the restless world of art and the lying world of literature—and the eagerness with which grace and despair quarrel to possess a generation of youth; but the majority of men usually fail in whatever is difficult and that therefore the ultimate spoiling of every enterprise of even a little elevation conforms to the custom of nature. Well! we shall rely upon grace. For if our tower stops half-way up or collapses above our heads, the foundations perhaps will have been well and truly laid.

13. Grace does not relieve the artist of his peculiar toil: it rather makes it more arduous by compelling him to bear a heavier burden. Now trees laden with fruit are bowed to the ground, but art must not stoop under its load.

No more does it relieve the Christian of human preparation and human effort, although it gives him, and because it gives him, both the will and the ability to perform. By ourselves alone we can do nothing, in no way add to the sum of being; but by ourselves alone we can do what is nothing, and diminish being. When the First Cause makes use of us as instruments, it is as animated instruments with free will, acted upon, no doubt, but at the same time acting. In the field of our free acts it also can do nothing without us. One moment of which man is master, in the most secret place of the heart, binds and looses eternity.

Mysticism is in fashion, asceticism less so. It is an appalling mistake to imagine that one can be separated from the other and its very certain laws. We cannot be half in love with Love. Our epoch feels itself too far gone not to cry out to Heaven—but at times as a sick man cries for morphia, not for health. Its cowardice provokes the fear that it may be pretending to serve two masters, setting its idiot hope in a radical division of the heart and the metaphysical annihilation of personality—as though the innumerable divisions, dissections and reduplications of physical phenomenology, however profound our weakness may suffer them to be in the whole range of indeliberate feelings and attractions and secondary choices, could affect the primitive choice of the will in a decision concerning its last end and the metaphysical essence of personality. We perceive in the end an abominable *counterfeit*, the diabolical collaboration of mysticism and sin, the Black Mass; so clearly that henceforth we shall expect the great danger of the age from a would-be religion and a would-be spirit, not from matter and "science."

The world from which the Saints formerly fled into the desert was no worse than ours. To describe our time, we should need to recall the first chapter of the Epistle to the Romans: "They have changed the truth of God into a lie, and worshipped and served the creature rather than the Creator . . . for this cause God delivered them up to

shameful affections. For their women have changed the
natural use into that use which is against nature . . ." and
the rest. The air we breathe is saturated with spiritual
filth and we have returned to the great night of the agony of
paganism, when man has to cope not only with his own
wretched body but with a body scourged by the angels of
Satan, when all nature clothes itself with obscene symbols, a
nightmare the obsession of which literary Freudism is everywhere busy multiplying. Would it not be foolhardy in the
extreme to try to work in such a world uncontaminated
without arming oneself with the strictest rules of ascetic
discipline? This is a case in which it is less tiring to run than
to walk.

It would be just as foolhardy to wait for infused knowledge instead of acquiring that which depends upon ourselves
—or what is worse, to despise knowledge. It must be
admitted that modern young people in general, victims of the
inhuman speeding-up imposed upon life, seem to lose heart
before a lengthy preparation of the mind. Alas! it is
expensive to neglect the mind. A reign of the heart which is
not first of all a reign of truth, a revival of Christianity which
is not first of all theological, disguises suicide in love. The age
is swarming with fools who look down upon reason. They
ought first to earn the right to speak ill of it. Love transcends
reason: what remains on this side is folly. Dazzled by
ecstasy and near to death, St. Thomas could say of the
Summa: "It seems to me rubbish": he had written it.

14. The simple-minded idolatry with which the majority
of artists worship their work, which becomes thrice sacred
once it has issued from their hands, is a proof of the essential
creative weakness of the human being. God does not adore
His works. Yet He knows them to be good. He does not
care about them, He lets man spoil them: even the gratuitous marvels of the supernatural order, charismata, pro-
phecies, miracles, the most innocent frolics of his poetry, are
as too lovely fireworks wasted in the night. But there is one
good which He does care about: souls, His special nourishment, the food of His love. Do you think that He would
weigh and compare man's greatest masterpiece with the least

degree of charity in a human soul ? Neither Art nor Poetry justifies the slightest act of rudeness towards Him.

There are, says St. Paul, some things which must not be so much as mentioned among you. Yet he immediately mentions them himself. What does that mean ? Nothing *by its kind alone* is a forbidden nutriment for art, like unclean animals to the Hebrews. From this point of view art can mention them all, as St. Paul mentions avarice and lechery. But on condition that, in the particular case and *in relation to the people* [185] it is aiming at and with whom it comes in contact, the work does not soil the mind and the heart. From this point of view if there are certain things which the artist is not strong enough or pure enough to mention without conniving with evil, he has no right to mention them. Let him wait a little. When he becomes a saint, he will be able to do as he likes.

What thanksgivings he would offer to morality, if he knew his own good ! By protecting his humanity, it indirectly protects his art as well. For however beautiful it may be in other respects, the work of art always ends by betraying, with infallible cunning, the vices of the workman [186]. The formal object of art is doubtless not in itself subordinate to the formal object of morality. Nevertheless, it is not only extrinsically and for the good of the human being that morality can influence the activity of the artist; it is concerned with this activity intrinsically as well—in the order of "material" and dispositive causality. For morality is not, as Kant would have it, a world of imperatives come down from the sky of liberty and foreign to the world of being. It takes its roots in the whole reality, of which it manifests a certain order of laws; not to acknowledge it is to diminish the real and so to impoverish the materials of art. An integral *realism* is only possible for an art sensitive to the whole truth of the universe of good and evil, for an art pervaded by the consciousness of grace and sin and the importance of the *moment* [187]. And all that is most real in the world escapes the notice of the darkened soul. "As one can say nothing about the beauties of the senses if one has not eyes to perceive them, so it is with the things of the spirit, if one cannot see how beautiful is the face of justice and temperance, and that neither the morning nor the evening star is so beautiful. We see them, when we have a soul capable of contemplating them and, seeing them, we experience a joy, an astonishment, a terror, stronger than before, because we are now in touch with true realities" [188].

There is only one way of freeing oneself from the law: to become one of the perfect, constantly influenced by the spirit of God, who have ceased to be under the law, doing by their own inclination what the law enjoins. So long as a man has not attained that goal—and does he ever attain it?—so long as he is not through grace one with the rule itself, he needs the restraining disciplines of morality to remain upright. He craves such a rod. And because the artist as such expresses himself and ought to express himself in his work as he is, then, if he is morally deformed, his art also, the intellectual virtue which is perhaps what is most sincere in him, runs the risk of receiving and deserving the birchings of morality. The conflict is inevitable. Man extricates himself as best he can, rather badly than well.

What makes the condition of modern art tragic is that it must be converted to find God again. And from the first conversion to the last, from baptism to the habit of virtue, there is a long way to go.   Would it be reasonable to expect some wavering, some disorder, some danger zones? It is natural for those who have the care of souls to take fright sometimes and to resort to severe measures; but they must, nevertheless, cherish the hope of the good things to come. If you talk to artists, tell them to make haste while they still have light, to fear Jesus who passes and does not return. If you talk to the prudent, tell them to be patient with poets, and to honour in the heart of man the longsuffering of God. But let them be vigilant to hate the filthy beast which prowls about poetry, that *literature* which, though a few real artists may escape its Hell, turns grace itself awry in many weaker ones, and changes divine things into a sham useful only to fatten fatuity.

15. Considering the human conditions which it presupposes, and the present state of hearts, the success of the hoped-for revival seems curiously problematical. It is like

a rose trying to blossom not on a dead branch, but on saw-dust.

I do not in the least pretend to say what will happen. I am not trying to discover what poets and novelists will be doing to-morrow. I am merely attempting to show how certain profound aspirations of contemporary art tend in the direction of a Christian Renaissance. I contemplate a possible future, what could be, what ought to be, if a man did not constantly betray his trust. It seems to me, then, that modern poetry, at any rate when it has not chosen despair, has for object in the sphere of art the very thing of which Our Lady is for ever in the order of sanctity the finished exemplar: doing common things in a divine way. This is just the reason why "to be a modern poet a man must be a great poet" [189]. At the end of an epoch when Nietzsche could point to "the general evolution of art in the direction of charla-tanry" [190], it is applying itself, still clumsily, to respect for genuine subordinations, to obedience, to sacrifice [191]. Wagner had led it astray; the example of Satie is teaching it once more a chaste honesty, a Stravinsky grandeur. After having pursued false purities so hard, it is on the way to the true. It is beginning to discover the secret significance of goodness and suffering and that "if the world has indeed, as I have said, been built of sorrow, it has been built by the hands of love," "for the secret of life is suffering. It is what is hidden behind everything" [192]. After such an orgy of sentimentalism, it wants rude contact with reality, stripped and naked. Now that so much literature and such an arro-gant initial confidence in enfranchised reason and the emanci-pated self have ended in the rupture manifest in Dadaism or in the free expressions of futurism (that dying breath of the past), it feels that it is its duty to piece together again, to reconcile the faculties of imagination and sensibility with religious knowledge, to recover "the whole man in the integral and indissoluble unity of his double nature" [193], the spiritual and the carnal, as in the intricacies of his nature and supernature, his life on earth and the mystery of the operations of Heaven. It foretells "the time of ardent grace" [194]; like contemplation, it would anticipate Heaven: "and let everything bear a new name."

It will not free itself from language or the work to be done, but it must make clear these intermediaries of the soul, and by dint of unremitting attention and self-denial make of matter such a channel of communication as will not distort or mutilate its message. And it is simplicity, as Julian Lanoë has well observed [195], which will give it precision and access to the depths. It will abandon, in order to cling to its object unalloyed, the delusive search for an ever-trifling and restricted originality; and an integrity, an instinct of disinterestedness, will open to it the mystery of universality.

Then the things of the spirit, which the tongues of men are powerless to tell, will find a means of expression. Art will no longer attempt in vain to violate the secrets of the heart; the heart will be held in such high honour that it will reveal its secrets spontaneously. What Rimbaud was unable to do, Love will. Where despair can go no farther, humility will pass. Where violence must be silent, charity will speak. Art will strew branches of palm-trees on the way of the Lord, before whom a choir of childish voices once sang the pious Hosanna.

"They gave You their praises when You were going to suffer: we give You our poetry in Your kingdom."

AN ESSAY ON ART

I. THE DIGNITY OF ART

WE are told by philosophers that the essence of art is not the performance of a moral act, but the making of some thing, some work, some object, with a view not to the human good of the agent, but to the requirements and proper good of the work to be done, by using means of realisation predetermined by the nature of the work in question.

Art so appears as something in itself outside the line of human conduct, something very nearly inhuman, whose requirements are nevertheless absolute, for, needless to say, there are not two ways of making an object well, of realising well the work conceived; there is only one, and it must not be missed.

Philosophers go on to say that this constructive activity is principally and above all an intellectual activity. Art is a virtue of the mind, a virtue of the practical mind, and may be described as the peculiar virtue of the working reasons.

But, it may be objected, if art is merely an intellectual virtue of construction, whence come the dignity and prestige it enjoys among mankind ? Why does this branch of our activity attract so much human energy ? Why has the poet at all times and among all nations been admired equally with the sage ?

The answer may in the first place be given that to create, to produce something intellectually, to manufacture an object *rationally constructed*, is a very considerable achievement in the world: in itself, for man, a way of imitating God. And here I mean art in general, as the Ancients understood it, the virtue of the artisan.

But where especially the maker of works becomes an imitator of God, where the virtue of art attains the nobility of absolute and self-sufficient things, is in that group of arts which by itself constitutes a whole spiritual world, namely the Fine Arts.

Two things are here to be considered. On the one hand, whatever be the nature and the ends in usefulness of the art under consideration, by its object it participates in something superhuman: for its object is the creation of beauty. Is not beauty a transcendental, a property of being, one of the Divine attributes? "The being of all things derives from the Divine Beauty," says St. Thomas. In that respect, then, the artist imitates God, Who created the world by communicating to it a likeness of His beauty.

. . . "The architect, by the disposition he knows,
Buildeth the structure of stone like a filter in the waters of
    the Radiance of God,
And giveth the whole building its sheen as to a pearl."

On the other hand, to create a work of beauty is to create a work resplendent with the glitter or the brilliance, the mystery of a *form*, in the metaphysical sense of the word, a radiance of intelligibility and truth, an irradiation of the primal effulgence. And the artist no doubt perceives this form in the world of creation, whether interior or exterior: he does not discover it complete in the sole contemplation of his creative mind, for he is not, like God, the cause of things. It is his eye and his mind that have perceived and disengaged it, and it must itself be alive within him, have assumed human life in him, live in his intelligence with an intellectual life and in his heart and flesh with a sensitive life, for him to be able to impart it to matter in the work he is doing.

The work so bears the stamp of the artist; it is the off-spring of his soul and mind.

In this respect also human art imitates God: it realises in the intellectual order, that is to say in the naturally most exalted order (I leave out of account the order of charity which is above it, being supernatural), it realises in action one of the fundamental aspects of the ontological resemblance of our soul to God.

It is indeed the ardent desire, the earnest prayer of the mind, taken in its pure state, to beget a living creature in its own likeness. And every mind utters a word: "To be fruitful enough to manifest what one has in oneself is a considerable perfection, pertaining essentially to the intellectual nature" [196]. Hence in the world of pure spirits, where there is no generation, there is the spiritual production of the mental word, in which the Angel coming to know his own nature reveals himself to himself, and by means of which he manifests what he knows to any other pure spirit he chooses. This mental word, to be sure, this spiritual utterance, remains a quality of the subject: it is not a substance, but a symbol. In creatures, the mind cannot succeed in producing in facsimile of nature another self, a subsisting person, it does not, properly speaking, engender; it makes an utterance, and that utterance is not an offspring. But this is owing to the essentially defective condition of the creature; the Mind itself, considered in its pure state, in its pure formal line, seeks to engender, to produce in self-knowledge something which shall not be a mere likeness, a symbol, an idea of the thing known, but the thing known itself existing for itself.

The Mind, the subsisting Mind, can fully realise in God alone, in the pure Act alone, the fundamental exigencies of its nature and give birth to *another self* at once substantial and personal, to a Word which shall be truly a Son. In the Holy Trinity alone do we see the coincidence of two functions which everywhere else are separate, the utterance of the Word and the generation of the Son, the Mind ending in a subsisting goal, in which the integrity of its own nature becomes substantially merged.

Well! We too, feeble though our mind be (it is on the lowest rung of spirits), ought to share in the nature of mind. For this reason the mind, despite the manifold defects peculiar to our species, strives to engender in us, is anxious to produce, not only the inner Word, the idea remaining inside us, but a work at once material and spiritual, like ourselves, with something of our soul over and above.

This requirement of the mind explains the presence of artists in our midst.

And you see that to establish fully the dignity and nobility of art, we have found it necessary to go back as far as the mystery of the Trinity.

It must, however, be carefully observed that our works of art are very far from being truly described as our children. They are inanimate things, they do not proceed from us *in similitudinem naturae,* they are the product of an artificial manufacture, not of a natural generation.

But be it observed that accidentally and in a certain relation, there is in the work of art something better answering the exigencies of the idea of generation: the great artist, I mean, is sure to put himself really into his work, is sure to stamp it with his own likeness, whereas in the case of a child, because of matter and heredity, it is not certainly the father or the mother, but any more or less desirable ancestor, who can come to life again and show his likeness. The father thinks he is himself again in his child; but it is the grandfather or the great-grandfather, the mother-in-law, who appears. There is in the child a fearful element of the unknown which is absent from the work of art. And it is understandable not that an artist should be more in love with his work than with his children, but that he should love them with a love almost as personal and from one point of view less anxious, and say when he thinks of them: "*Not all of me will die.*"

II. GRATUITOUSNESS

Considerations such as these show that art, as such, is *gratuitous* or disinterested. That is to say, that in the actual production of the work the virtue of art has only one object, the good of the work to be done; to make matter resplendent with beauty, to create a thing in accordance with the laws of its being, independently of anything else. At the same time its desire is that there shall be nothing in the work eluding its control, that it alone shall regulate the work directly, handle and shape it.

There are many ways of failing to attain this "gratuitousness." A man may think, for example, that excellent moral intentions may make up for deficiencies in the quality of the craft or the inspiration, and are sufficient for the construction of a work. Or a man might go so far as to alter the work itself as the rules and the determined ways of art required it to be, by the forcible application, to control it, of alien elements—a desire to edify or to disedify, not to outrage the public, or to provoke a scandal, to have "arrived" in society, or to cut a figure in bars and cafés as an *artist* free and rare. . . .

You see what meaning has to be given to the theory of the gratuitousness of art: that the virtue of art which the artist uses, whatever other end it may serve, shall by itself aim only at the perfection of the work and suffer no control over the work which does not come through it.

But this doctrine and the word "gratuitousness" are often understood in a quite different and much more ambitious sense. They are made to mean not only what I have just said but also that art ought to enjoy *in man* and *among men* an absolute independence, that it ought to tolerate no human interest or any superior law in the artist, absolutely nothing outside the sole concern of artistic manufacture; which comes to saying that the man who is also an artist ought to be an artist only—and therefore ought not to be a man. But if there is no man there can be no artist: by devouring humanity, art destroys itself. This was what Baudelaire termed *The Pagan School.* "Absorbed," he wrote, "by the fierce passion for whatever is beautiful, comic, pretty or picturesque, for there are degrees, the ideas of what is right and true disappear. The frenzied passion for art is a cancer which eats up everything else. . . . Excessive specialisation of a faculty ends in nothing."

.   .   .   .   .

It seems to me that this erroneous conception of the gratuitousness of art can assume two special forms.

There is first, rather through opposition to romanticism, the idea of gratuitousness proclaimed by the Parnassians, then by the Symbolists and Mallarmé, and perhaps also, in a different sphere, by Max Jacob, Erik Satie and their school (some of them have since abandoned such a position). The content of the work of art, the material to be shaped, the artistic *thing*, the lyrical and intellectual stuff, are all an irksome burden, an impurity to be got rid of. Pure art, in

short, involves nothing, the subject being completely
whittled away. I call that a sin of idealism in relation to
the *matter* of art: pushed to the extreme, a perfect building,
with nothing to build.

After the exasperation of sensibility provoked by impressionism, after that din of noisy claims, those wonders,
evocations, swoons and psychological shivers, such an idea
of gratuitousness may have been a purifying and beneficent
phase in serving to remind us that the essential in art is the
control imposed by mind upon matter. In this sense Georges
Auriac has very appositely observed: "*A tight-rope walker
and a dancer* are the two creatures combined in every artist
who moves me. Every new work is a tight-rope stretched
above an everlasting track. . . . Even to-day, you can
realise how very cautiously artists like Stravinsky and Satie
have to cross the wire which is to be their only way." Nevertheless the theory of gratuitousness, understood in the
crude meaning I have deliberately given to it, is false,
precisely because it leaves out of account the very matter
of artistic control and the indispensable part it plays.

No doubt, if there is next to no matter, the work of the
artist will more easily succeed. But art, as has been sufficiently dinned into our ears, ought not to be on the look out
for what is easy. It must have opposition and constraint,
the constraint of rules and the opposition of matter. The
more obstinate and rebellious the matter, the better will art,
by its success in mastering it, realise its own end, which is to
make matter resplendent with a dominating intelligibility.
This has been well expressed by André Gide: "Art is always
the result of some constraint. To think that it rises higher
in proportion as it is free, is to think that what keeps the kite
from climbing the sky is the string to which it is attached.
Kant's dove, which thought it would be able to fly better
without that wind keeping its wings back, fails to realise that
for it to be able to fly at all, it needs the resistance of the air
on which to lean its wings. . . . Art longs for liberty only
in times of sickness: it would like to exist easily. Whenever
it feels itself strong, it looks for struggle and obstacles. It
likes to burst its bonds and therefore prefers them tight."

.   .   .   .   .

But the theory of the gratuitousness of art can give rise to another more specious error, and it is Gide himself this time who suggests it. "The artist," we are told, "is asked in only after dinner. His task is to provide not food, but intoxication." And he adopts Renan's remark: "To be able to think freely, a man must be certain that no consequences will follow whatever he writes," whence it follows that every thinker taking into account the consequences of his writings does not think freely. "Are you interested in moral questions?" he makes an imaginary interlocutor ask him. "What!" he replies, "the very stuff of my books!" "Then what is morality, according to you?" "A branch of Æsthetics." Oscar Wilde had remarked pretty much in the same sense but with greater dignity of expression: "The highest Art rejects the burden of the human spirit."

That is to say, the theory of gratuitousness, in reaction against exclusively moralist or apologetic or civic pre-occupations considered as "utilitarian," now no longer requires the *matter* of art to be whittled away, but the elimination of every *human end* pursued. Let the artist take for stuff and substance of his work whatever is most profound, most exalted and most vile, the moral life of man, the heart of man "hollow and full of filth"—and the rarest passions and the life of the spirit itself, nay, the Gospel and sanctity, everything; but with it all an absolute prohibition, upon pain of committing a sacrilege against art, against pursuing any other end than the pure delight, order, riches, tranquillity and rapture, which the soul ought to savour in the work. This is no longer art *on nothing* as in the theory of gratuitousness in its first form; but art *for nothing*, for nothing but art's sake.

The theory of gratuitousness, in this second guise, is singularly specious, because it exploits and distorts a very real truth touching the intimate nature of art which we should be careful not to misconceive. It is nevertheless a very noxious poison, which must in the long run exercise a completely sterilising effect upon art.

Precisely because, given a work of a certain kind to be done, there are strictly determined ways of realising it, depending upon the pure exigencies of the work itself and brooking no liberties, the virtue of art, as I have just mentioned, will not have the work interfered with and directly controlled by anything other than itself; it insists that it alone shall touch the work and keep contact with it to bring it into being. In short, art requires that nothing shall attain the work but *through itself as intermediary*. This is the element of truth in the theory of gratuitousness. Woe to the artist who fails to meet this insistence of his art, a jealous, fierce insistence, like every insistence of the mind and its virtues. Here again we can discover in our art as it were a trace of the Blessed Trinity. *The Word*, says St. Augustine, *is in a way the art of Almighty God*. And by the Word the whole divine work was done, *omnia per ipsum facta sunt*. It is through His Word and His art that God attains, controls and realises, everything He does. And in the same way it is *through his art* that the human artist ought to attain, control and realise, all his work.

But does that prove that the work depends on the art alone, and not on the whole soul of the artist; that it is made by the art alone, separate, cut off from all the rest in man, and not by man the artist with every human will and every human thought he has in his heart, every election he makes, every end he pursues, every higher law which he would have himself obey? Far from it! It is as though, on the pretext that everything has been created by the Word, we were to say that the world, having been created *per Verbum*, had not been created by the whole undivided Trinity. Gratuitously no doubt, and the only instance of absolutely gratuitous art, absolutely free from the least interested intention. But to an end nevertheless, an end which was not simply the perfection of the work to be achieved; an end which was of an order superior to the art—the communication of the divine Goodness.

The theorists of gratuitousness omit an elementary distinction, omit to distinguish the *art*, which, as such, has no other end than the good of the thing to be made, from the *artist*, who, as working man, can have as many ends as he pleases. And they omit this commonsense distinction because they fail to take into account a more subtle distinction, the distinction between the "principal agent" and the "instrumental cause," between the workman and the instrument. An invisible and intangible activity is transmitted through the instrument wielded by the worker, making the instrument produce a nobler effect than itself and really produce the whole work, but in a subordinate capacity. So the picture is wholly of the brush and wholly of the painter; there is nothing, absolutely nothing, in it but proceeds from the brush, and nothing in it but proceeds from the painter.

This distinction plays a capital part in metaphysics; it alone enables one to understand how the free act of the creature is wholly of the creature as a secondary cause, and, if it is a good act, wholly of God as a primary cause: God makes the will do it in the will's own way, that is to say freely. Philosophers who do not admit this distinction are forced to consider the divine action as interfering to interpolate some alien element or other into human liberty, some rival element which would mar its purity. André Gide makes a similar mistake. He does not see that the virtue of art, with all its perfection and peculiar exigencies, is an *instrument* in relation to the artist, the principal agent. The soul of the artist with all its human fullness, with every object of its love and worship, all the intentions, human, moral and religious, outside the artistic order which it can pursue, is the principal cause, using the virtue of art as an instrument; and so the work is wholly of the soul and the will of the artist as principal cause, and wholly of his art as instrument, without the artist losing a tittle of his mastery over matter and his integrity, his purity and ingenuousness—just as our good acts are wholly ours secondarily and wholly God's primarily, without on that account being any the less free.

This does not mean a juxtaposition of two forces each pulling a different way. The virtue of art is instrumentally subordinate to the soul which acts by means of it. The greater the artist, the more vigorous his art, neither stooping nor bent, but erect and imperious, the more successful will the man be in passing completely into his work by means of his art. Diminish the man in the artist, you necessarily diminish the art itself, which is of the man. The theory of gratuitousness in its second guise is another idealist heresy. It misconceives not the *matter* of the work of art, but the *human subject* of whom the virtue of art is a quality.

If the artist has not taken sides in the great debate between angels and men, if he is not convinced that his contribution, while including pleasure, is nourishment and not intoxication only, his work will always remain in some aspects defective and mean. The greatest poets, and the most disinterested, the most "gratuitous," had some message for mankind. Is it not the case of Dante, Cervantes, Racine, Shakespeare, Goethe, Baudelaire and Dostoievsky? Whatever Dostoievsky's doctrine may be, his heart is Christian: Gide, who could discern in him only his own features, has sadly erred in regard to Dostoievsky. How reasonable, may it be once more observed from this point of view, how little "immoralist," are Goethe's explanations in *Dichtung und Wahrheit* of the origin of *Werther!* And what a tragically religious anxiety under his mask of dandyism Baudelaire reveals in *Mon coeur mis à nu!*

Is not the art of La Fontaine an eminent example of *gratuitous* art? But as Henri Ghéon observed to Valéry: "if there were not lacking to it a grain of spirituality, a tinge of Christianity, the art of such a fabulist would be the art of the *apologist*, the type of *edifying* art."

True, it may be said. But supposing La Fontaine had acquired this grain of spirituality without ceasing to be La Fontaine, the La Fontaine we know; in exercising his apologist's art he would never have been consumed by a zeal for souls and the apostolate. "If Jammes and Claudel are Christian artists, it is not because of their intense and distinctive devotion. The apostolate is never an æsthetic virtue" [197]. More generally, does it not seem that the happiest conditions for the artist are conditions of peace and spiritual order in and around him, that having his soul in order and orientated towards its last end, he should thereafter have no other anxiety than to do his job well and set himself free—such as he is—in his work, without another thought, without pursuing any particular and predetermined human end? Was that not exactly how the artists of the Middle Ages went to work? And in our time a Cézanne?

To such an objection—which is not lacking in force and concedes the essential—I have two answers to make. In the first place, if it be true that the task is more difficult, the danger of giving way greater, for the worker who pursues in his work a particular and predetermined end of a human sort—a Lucretius eager to spread the philosophy of Epicurus, a Virgil undertaking the *Georgics* to bring labour back to the land, or a Wagner intent on the glorification of the Teutonic religion—the danger nevertheless is not insurmountable, the task not impossible, as witness the names just quoted.

In the second place, and most important of all, those who by their art desire to serve the Truth which is Christ are not pursuing a particular human end but a divine end, an end as universal as God Himself. The more they live their faith, the more spiritual their inner life becomes, the more deeply rooted they are in the Church, the higher do they rise above human limitations and the conventions, opinions, and special interests of particular social groups; so that, with a fuller understanding of the pure spirituality and universality of the action of God in their souls, their art and their thoughts are purged of all human narrowness, to be thenceforth concentrated upon the boundless Love which is and acts on earth as in Heaven. This is what men who are utterly ignorant of the Faith or deceived by an excess of appearances are incapable of understanding; in zeal for souls they see merely a human effort at domination, an attempt to serve the interest of some sect or clique. They cannot see that those who take part as Christians, because they are Christians, in the works of the mind, are not engaged in *clerical* philosophy or *clerical* art, or in *confessional* philosophy or *confessional* art. There is in this sense no Catholic philosophy or Catholic art, for Catholicism is not a *particular statement of faith* any more than it is *a* religion: it is *the* religion, confessing the only omnipresent Truth. Yet their art and philosophy are Catholic, that is to say genuinely universal.

I would add that man always serves some master and that the devil is not the least exacting overlord. In forbidding man to pursue any other end than art itself, you are, whatever you may do, positively appointing a last end for him, a god: Art in person. You are binding him to a religion much more tyrannical than the true religion. You are delivering him up to æsthetic clericalism, assuredly the most pernicious of all forms of clericalism.

A man like Gide seems to me to be living under a perpetual constraint, cribbed, cabined and confined by inexorable conventions, never free, never spontaneous: for ever haunted by morality. A moral choice confronts him at every corner of the street, and he will be compelled to make an election: quick, he must escape, escape far away! What torture!

Only the artist who consents to be a man, who is not afraid of morality, who is not every moment terrified of losing the flower of his ingenuousness, enjoys the real gratuitousness of art. He is what he is, careless of what he may appear to be; he affirms if he wants to affirm, he believes, loves, chooses, gives himself, follows his inclination and his fancy, recreates and amuses himself, enjoys himself playing.

III. OF A TOO HUMAN ANTINOMY

Truth to tell, I believe it to be impossible outside Catholicism to reconcile in man, without diminishing or forcing them, the rights of morality and the claims of intellectuality, art or science. Morality as such aims only at the good of the human being, the supreme interests of the acting Subject; Intellectuality as such aims only at the Object, its nature, if it is to be known, what it ought to be, if it is to be made. What a temptation for poor human nature to be faithful to one only at the expense of the other! True, we know, *haec oportebat facere, et illa non omittere ;* but how shall the children of Adam keep the balance? Outside the Church and its divine life it is natural that moral and religious zeal should turn man against the mind, and it is natural that zeal for art and science should turn man away from the eternal laws. Socrates's judges, Luther, Rousseau, Tolstoi, and the Anglo-Saxon pragmatists, are in one camp: in the other Bruno, Bacon, the great pagans of the Renaissance, Goethe himself, and Nietzsche.

Catholicism orders our whole life to Truth itself and subsisting Beauty. In us it places the theological virtues above the moral and intellectual virtues and, through them, gives us peace. *Et ego si exaltatus fuero, omnia traham ad meipsum.* Christ crucified draws to Himself everything there is in man: all things are reconciled, but at the height of His heart.

Here is a religion whose moral exigencies are more elevated than those of any other, inasmuch as only the heroism of sanctity can fully satisfy them, and which at the same time more than any other admires and protects the mind. I say it is a sign of the divine origin of that religion. A superhuman virtue is necessary to secure the free play of art and science among men under the supremacy of the divine law and the primacy of Charity and so to realise the higher reconciliation of the *moral* and the *intellectual.*

SOME REFLECTIONS UPON
RELIGIOUS ART

ALLOW me to put before you to-day some very short and simple reflections. You will, no doubt, consider them too simple—but I hope they are inspired by common sense.

What I should like to examine with you very rapidly is the present state of relations between Catholic artists and the Catholic public. We must first observe that there is in general mutual dissatisfaction; and, as in family quarrels, we must no doubt say that there are "faults on both sides," that each party has good grounds for complaint.

Everything that can be has been said on what is called the *art of St. Sulpice* (the term is ill chosen, and very insulting to an estimable Parisian parish, the more so because the plague is world-wide); on the devilish ugliness, an offence to God and much more harmful than is generally believed to the spread of religion, of the great bulk of contemporary objects manufactured for the decoration of churches; on the kind of bitter contempt still prevalent, in some "respectable" circles, for artists and poets; lastly on the lack of taste and artistic education which arouses an earnest desire for the establishment in seminaries of such courses of æsthetics or the history of art as H.H. Pius XI had, before his elevation to the Pontificate, organised at Milan.

Yes, indeed: but there are on the other hand many parish priests sincerely desirous of fulfilling the wish of Pius X, "to make their people pray upon beauty," and anxious to rid their churches of the products belched out of the cellars of religious commerce. Many of these, it must be candidly admitted, are far from satisfied with what is offered to them in the name of modern art. I am clearly not referring to a few distinguished works, but to the *average* produced in the last few years. Now affection for one's friends should not prevent one—rather the opposite—from noticing what may still be lacking in an effort which in other respects commands our heartiest admiration. Such parish priests, I say, are often right, for their business undoubtedly is not to patronise the Fine Arts, but to give the faithful what answers their spiritual needs, what really can be of *use* to the religious life of a Christian community. We sometimes see them driven back in despair on the art of St. Sulpice. And why? Because these products of commercial manufacture, when they are not too heart-breaking, have at any rate the advantage of being absolutely indeterminate, so colourless, so devoid of significance that they can be looked at without being seen, and receive our own feelings, whereas some modern works, especially the most tortured and impassioned, claim to impose upon us by violence in their crude state, and as subjectively as may be, the individual emotions of the artist himself. And it is an intolerable nuisance in saying one's prayers, instead of finding oneself before a representation of Our Lord or some Saint, to receive full in the chest, with the force of a blow, the religious sensibility of Mr. So-and-So.

The difficulties of the present day, to tell the truth, arise from deepset causes and, ultimately, from the crisis affecting our whole civilisation. Religious art is not a thing which can be isolated from art simply, from the general artistic movement of an age: confine it, and it becomes corrupted, its expression a dead letter. On the other hand the art of a period carries with it all the intellectual and spiritual stuff which constitutes the life of the period; and in spite of whatever rare and superior qualities contemporary art may possess in the order of sensibility, virtue and invention, the spirituality it conveys is not infrequently poor indeed and sometimes very corrupt.

This is the reason why Christian artists are faced by very grave difficulties. They must on the one hand reaccustom the faithful to beauty, whose taste has been spoiled for more than a century past—and we must not forget that, given the purpose it is intended to serve, religious art, as prescribed by Urban VIII on March 15, 1642, and the canons of the Council of Trent, must not have an "unwonted" character—and so it is a question of destroying bad æsthetic habits, while re-establishing one good one—no easy task. On the other hand, to recover a really live religious art, it is the whole of modern art that they have to elevate, spiritualise, and lead to the feet of God—and that is not an easy task. Truly by that very fact the Christian artist, if he have the genius, is in a privileged position to profit by the whole modern effort.

What is the upshot of all this ? It is quite clear that the Catholic public would fall short of an essential duty of special urgency if it failed to understand the capital importance of the task undertaken with admirable generosity by so many artists working to reintroduce sensible beauty into the House of God, if it did not effectively support them, and if, even when not approving of any particular work, it did not surround them with a fraternal sympathy. But it is also plain that Catholic artists on their side ought to make an effort to understand the legitimate needs of the faithful, for whose common good they are working, and courageously take account of the special conditions and exigencies of the task to which they are devoting themselves.

But, I may be asked, cannot some of these conditions be stated ? I think, at all events, that a few self-evident elementary truths concerning religious art can be discerned which, if universally recognised, would undoubtedly facilitate an understanding between the public and artists. Allow me, if you please, to state some on which, I fancy, all here are agreed, and which are commonly admitted by all our friends.

First Observation. There is no style *peculiar* to religious art, there is no *religious technique*. Anyone who believes in the existence of a religious technique is on the high road to Beuron. If it is true that not all styles are alike suited to sacred art, it is still more true that sacred art, as I said a moment ago, cannot isolate itself, that it must, at all times, following the example of God Himself who speaks the language of men, assume, the while exalting them from within, every means and every form of technical vitality, so to speak, placed at its disposal by the contemporary generation. (From this point of view, it may be parenthetically observed, it does not seem at all necessary that Christian artists, especially such as have not attained to full possession of their craft, should work in sacred art exclusively. Let them begin by doing still-life studies, accustom themselves to discovering a religious significance in the inevitable apples, jam-jar, pipe and mandolin.)

There are nevertheless two conditions, I think, in the technical order necessary to religious art as such, granted its special object and the purpose it is intended to serve.

1. It must be *intelligible*. For *it is there above all for the instruction of the people, it is a theology in graphic representation*. An unintelligible, obscure, Mallarméan religious art is about as absurd as a house without a staircase or a cathedral without a porch.

2. The work must be *finished*. I do not mean finished in the academic sense, but in the most material and humble meaning of the word. It is in the highest degree fitting that nothing shall enter the house of God but work which is well done, accomplished, clean, permanent and honest. *This must clearly be understood according to the peculiar style of the work and the means taken to achieve it*, but the ease with which in our day artists are satisfied with themselves compels me to insist upon this point.

Second Observation. Sacred art is in a state of absolute dependence upon theological wisdom. There is manifested in the figures it sets before our eyes something far above all our human art, divine Truth itself, the treasure of light purchased for us by the blood of Christ. For this reason chiefly, because the sovereign interests of the Faith are at stake in the matter, the Church exercises its authority and magistracy over sacred art. I mentioned a moment ago the decree of Urban VIII of March 15, 1642, and the enactment of the 25th session of the Council of Trent. There are other instances. On June 11, 1623, the Congregation of Rites prohibited a crucifix representing Christ with arms updrawn. On September 11, 1670, a decree of the Holy Office forbade the making of crucifixes "in such a vulgar and artless way, in such an indecent attitude, with features so tortured with grief as to provoke disgust rather than pious regard." And you are aware that in March, 1921, the Holy Office forbade the exhibition in churches of certain works by the Flemish painter Servaes.

Here is a point deserving all our attention. Servaes is a painter of very considerable talent, a Christian full of faith, and one can only speak of his character with respect and friendly feeling. I am happy to bear witness to it here. *The Stations of the Cross* which raised such a violent commotion in Belgium stirred deep religious emotions in certain souls, nay, brought about conversions. The work in itself is beautiful and worthy of admiration. Nevertheless the Church condemned it, and it is never difficult, even when appearances and human methods of procedure disconcert us, to understand the wisdom and the excellent reasons behind the decisions of the Church. In spite of himself, assuredly, and not in his soul but in his work, the painter, fascinated by the *Ego sum vermis et non homo* of Isaias and conceiving his *Via Crucis* as the very dizziness of grief, found himself falsifying certain theological truths of capital importance—above all the truth that the sufferings, like the death of Our Lord, were essentially voluntary, and that it was a divine Person who suffered the most appalling human suffering: the pain and agony of His Humanity were handled by the Word as a tool with which It performed Its great work. At the same time, for such as cannot harmonise the poor symbols which Art sets before their eyes and the pure image living in our hearts of the most beautiful of the children of men (for in His case, as in His Mother's, as Cajetan reminds us in his essay *De Spasmo beatae Virginis*, the supreme torments of Calvary, piercing the mind still more cruelly than the body, yet left His reason intact upon the Cross in the full exercise of its dominion over the senses)— for such, I say, certain plastic distortions, a sort of degenerate aspect of the outline, are tantamount to an insult to the Humanity of the Saviour and, as it were, a doctrinal misconception of the sovereign dignity of His soul and body.

At a time when the truth of the Faith is threatened on all sides, should we be surprised that the Church should be more than ever concerned at the distortions of doctrine which may be implicit in certain works of art intended for the use of the faithful, whatever their æsthetic value otherwise may be and the salutary emotions they may in some cases excite, and whatever the piety, faith, depth of spiritual life and highmindedness of the artist who wrought them?

I would nevertheless like to add that from this same

dogmatic point of view, the disgraceful sentimentality of so many commercial products must be an equal source of distress to sound theology, and is tolerated no doubt only as one of the abuses to which we resign ourselves from time to time having regard to human weakness and to what may be described as, adapting a phrase of Holy Writ, "the infinite number of Christians with bad taste."

This last-mentioned ultimate control by theology, which presupposes in the artist a genuine theological culture, clearly does not impose any æsthetic *genre*, any style, any particular technique, on sacred art. We must, however, realise that it gives it, as it were spontaneously, certain general directions. For instance, the intrinsic characteristics of the object represented are assuredly of very special importance for sacred art; not from the point of view of naturalist imitation of material details and picturesque appearances, which are more out of place and execrable here than elsewhere, but from the point of view of the laws of *intellectual significance*. Considering the essential inadequacy of the means of expression of human art in relation to the divine mysteries to which they are applied, the frightful difficulty of expressing in a sensitive medium truths which cleave the earth and sky and unite the most opposed realities, one would even be inclined to think that sacred art, however rich it ought to be in sensibility and humanity, ought undoubtedly, if it is to attain a certain spiritual fullness, to retain always some element of hieratic and so to speak ideographical symbolism, and, in any event, of the strong intellectuality of its primitive traditions.

Third (and last) Observation. Merely this, that a work of religious art ought to be religious. If it is not religious, it is not *beautiful*, for beauty presupposes essentially the integrity of all the requisite conditions. As Paul Cazin remarked, tell an artist handling a religious subject "that he has produced a masterpiece, but that his masterpiece is not religious, and you will give him pain . . ." Cazin goes on: "God alone can touch men's hearts with a feeling of piety before the tawdriest chromolithograph, the most heart-breaking daub, as much as before the most sublime masterpiece." That is true, but it does not prevent certain works of art from having normally a value *in themselves*, a radiation of religious emotion, of interior illumination and, specifically, of sanctification. Nevertheless, let us repeat once more after Maurice Denis, this does not depend on the *subject* itself. Nor does it depend, I am convinced, on the formula of a school and a particular technique. It would be a great mistake to think that clumsy angles and a cheap material are the necessary means of expressing a Franciscan emotion or that a geometrical rigidity and dull, austere tones are required to stamp a work with the seal of Benedictine dignity.

There are no rules for giving an artistic object the value of a religious emotion. This depends on a certain interior freedom in regard to rules. It can be achieved only by not being directly pursued, and by the artist sharing, in one way or another, in the spiritual life of the Saints. This was made easy for artists by the common Christian atmosphere of the ages of faith, even when they kept themselves far removed, from many points of view, from the examples of the Saints; but of itself, and lacking such exterior assistance, it requires in the soul the habitual radiation of the theological virtues and supernatural wisdom. It is, moreover, essential that the virtue of art do not remain separate, isolated from such wisdom, because of an imperfect mastery or misleading academic principles, but that the two be put in contact, the virtue of art freely employing such wisdom as a supple and infallible instrument.

NOTES

1. By wisdom is here meant Wisdom, as *a manner of knowledge*, Metaphysics and Theology. The Schoolmen distinguish a higher wisdom, wisdom as *a manner of inclination* or *connaturality with divine things*. This wisdom, which is one of the gifts of the Holy Ghost, does not stop at knowledge, but knows by loving and for loving. "The object of the contemplation of Philosophers is the perfection of him who contemplates, and therefore their contemplation stops in the intellect and so their end in this is the knowledge of the intellect. But the object of the contemplation of the Saints, sc. of Catholics, is love of the object contemplated, sc. God: therefore it does not stop in the intellect as an ultimate end through knowledge, but passes over to affection through love." (Albert the Great (Jean de Castel), *De adhaerendo Deo.* cap ix.)

2. "A practical end is necessary, because 'practical people,' that is to say artisans, although they aim at knowing what the truth is in respect of divers matters, do not pursue it as an ultimate end. For they do not consider the cause of truth in itself, and for itself, but by way of ordering it to the end of the operation or of applying it to some definite particular object and some definite time." (St. Thomas, in lib. ii, *Metaph.*, lect. 2; Aristotle, *Metaph.* ii, c. 1, 995 b 21.)

3. Cf. John of St. Thomas, *Cursus Philos.*, Log. ii, q. 1. *Cursus Theol.* (Vivès, t. vi), q. 62, disp. 16, a. 4.

4. Artistic work therefore is specifically human work as opposed to the work of the beast or the machine; and for this reason human production is in its normal state an *artisan's* production, and therefore necessitates a strict individual appropriation. For the artist as such can share nothing in common; in the line of moral aspirations there must be a communal use of goods, whereas in the line of production the same goods must be objects of particular ownership. Between the two horns of this antinomy St. Thomas places the social problem.

When work becomes *inhuman* or *sub-human*, because its artistic character is effaced and matter gets the better of man, the material factors of civilisation, left to themselves, naturally tend to communism and the death of production, through the very excess of proprietarism and productivism which is brought about by the predominance of the *factibile*.

5. Prudence on the other hand is the undeviating determination of acts to be done (*recta ratio agibilium*), and Science the undeviating determination of the objects of speculation (*recta ratio speculabilium*).

6. To simplify the exposition, only such *habits* are here intended as *perfect* the subject; there are also habitual dispositions (e.g. vices) which incline the subject *to evil*. The Latin word *habitus* is much less expressive than the Greek word, ἕξις but it would be pedantic currently to use the latter term. For this reason and for lack of a suitable English equivalent, I have retained *habit* in the text, and beg to be excused the use of such a clumsy expression. [ἕξις, as Professor Burnet points out (cf. *The Ethics of Aristotle*, Methuen & Co., London, 1900), is a term borrowed from the vocabulary of medicine and gymnastics. The τελείωσις, "completion," of any ἕξις is its ἐνέργεια, "activity." ἕξις is distinguished in the Categories 9 a. 8 from διάθεσις as being more permanent. Knowledge and goodness are ἕξεις, health and disease are διαθέσεις. Consider ἕξις, then, as "form" or "condition" of an athlete or a race-horse.]

7. Such habits perfecting the very nature of being and not the faculties are called *entitative habits*.

8. *Natural* habits are here intended, not *supernatural* habits (infused moral virtues, theological virtues, gifts of the Holy Ghost), which are *infused* and not *acquired*.

9. Through failing to make this distinction, Ravaisson, in his famous essay on Habit, spread dense clouds of Leibnizian smoke over the philosophy of Aristotle.

10. Cf. Cajetan, in ii–ii, q. 171, a 2.

11. Aristotle, *de Coelo*, lib. i.

12. *Sum. Theol.*, i–ii, q. 55, a. 3.

13. *Ibid.*, a. 2, *ad* 1: *Unumquodque enim quale est, tale operatur.*

14. Cf. Cajetan, in i–ii, q. 57, a 5, *ad* 3: John of St. Thomas, *Cursus Theol.* (t. vi), q. 62, disp. 16, a 4. "The function of the

practical intellect is to measure the work to be done and regulate it. And so its truth lies not in being, but in what ought to be according to the rule and the measure for regulating the thing in question."

15. John of St. Thomas, *Curs. Phil.*, Log. ii, q. 1, a. 5.

16. So St. Augustine defines virtue as *ars recte vivendi* (*de Civ. Dei*, lib. IV, cap. 21). Cf. on this point Aristotle, *Eth. Nic.*, vi; St. Thomas, *Sum. Theol.*, ii–ii, q. 47, a. 2, *ad* 1; i–ii, q. 21, a. 2, *ad* 2: q. 57, a. 4, *ad* 3.

17. "If you must have works of art, are not those who model in human clay the likeness of God's own features to be preferred to Phidias?" (P. Gardeil, *Les dons du Saint Esprit dans les Saints Dominicains*, Lecoffre, 1903, Introd., pp. 23–4.)

18. *Isaias* xl. 31: "*They that hope in the Lord shall renew their strength: they shall take wings as eagles: they shall run, and not be weary: they shall walk and not be faint.*" "Hereupon it may be pertinently observed," adds John of St. Thomas (*Cursus Theol.*, t. vi, q. 70, disp. 18, a. 1), "that the wings of an eagle are promised; but it is not said that they will fly, but that they will run and walk, like men still living on earth, impelled, however, and driven by the wings of an eagle swooping down from on high, because the gifts of the Spirit, although they are exercised on earth and seem to take place in accustomed acts, are none the less directed by the wings of an eagle which are impelled and controlled by the communication of more exalted spirits and gifts: and those who are moved by ordinary virtues are as different from those who are impelled by the gifts of the Holy Ghost as those who walk painfully on their own feet, controlled by their own effort and industry, differ from those who, moved by the wings of an eagle filled with a wind from on high, run in the way of the Lord with no apparent effort."

19. *Sum. Theol.*, i–ii, q. 57, a. 3.

20. *Ibid.*, q. 21, a. 2, *ad* 2. "The fact of a man being a poisoner is nothing against his prose." Oscar Wilde, "Pen, Pencil and Poison," in *Intentions* (Methuen & Co., London).

21. "And therefore it is not a necessity of art that the artisan work well, but that he turn out good work: there would, however,

be a greater necessity that the product of the art perform its function well, that a knife, e.g., should cut well, and a saw saw well, if the peculiarity of these was to act and not rather to be passive, because they have no control over their acts." *Sum. Theol.*, i–ii, q. 57, a. 5, *ad* 1.

In contrasting (in *Bedenken von Aufrichtung*, etc., Klopp, I, 133 et seq.) the inferiority of Italian art, "which has confined itself almost exclusively to making things which are lifeless, motionless, and good to look upon from outside," with the superiority of German art, which has from the beginning devoted itself to making works which move (watches, clocks, hydraulic machines, etc.), Leibniz, that great man who shone in everything except Æsthetics, had a presentiment of a truth, but unfortunately confused the *motus ab intrinseco* of a clock with that of a living being.

22. *Sum. Theol.*, i–ii, q. 57, a. 4.

23. Aristotle, *Eth. Nic.*, vi. Cf. Cajetan, in i–ii, q. 58, a. 5.

24. Cf. *Sum. Theol.*, i–ii, q. 57, a. 1; q. 21, a. 2, *ad* 2.

25. *Eth. Nic.*, vi, 5.

26. *Sum. Theol.*, i–ii, q. 47, a. 8. "He is a poor master," noted Leonardo da Vinci, "whose work surpasses his judgement: he alone is advancing towards the perfection of art whose judgement surpasses his work." (*Textes Choisis*, published by Péladan, Paris, 1907, § 403.)

27. "What things conduce to the end in human affairs are not determined, but susceptible of infinite variety according to the diversity of people and their occupations." *Sum. Theol.*, ii–ii, q. 47, a. 15.

28. It goes without saying that as far as the precepts of the moral law are concerned, all cases are identical *in this sense*, that such precepts ought always to be obeyed. But there are individual differences in moral cases as to the *modalities* of the conduct to be observed in conformity with the said precepts.

29. St. Thomas, *in Poster. Analyt.* lib. i, lect. 1, 1.

30. John of St. Thomas, *Cursus Theol.* (t. vi), q. 62, disp. 16, a. 4.

31. "The practical intellect in relation to (*in ordine ad*) an undeviating will." (*Sum. Theol.*, i–ii, q. 56, a. 3.)

32. Cf. Ch. VI, "The Rules of Art," pp. 47–49.

33. John of St. Thomas, *loc. cit.*

33*b*. In this sense a poet has been able to say: "Art is science incarnate" (Jean Cocteau, *Le Secret Professionnel*); and a painter: "Art is merely humanised science" (Gino Severini, *Du Cubisme au Classicisme*), so rejoining the ancient idea of *scientia practica*. [Cf. D. V. Fumet's "Art is a mathematics of the heart," quoted in Stanislas Fumet's *Le Procès de l'Art*, Plon, Paris, 1929, p. 137.]

34. *Sum. Theol.*, i–ii, q. 57, a. 4, *ad* 2.

35. Cf. Aristotle, *Metaph.*, i, c. 1: St. Thomas, lect. 1, §§ 20–2; St. Thomas, *Sum. Theol.*, ii–ii, q. 47, a. 3, *ad* 3; q. 49, a. 1, *ad* 1; Cajetan, in i–ii, q. 57, a. 4; in ii–ii, q. 47, a. 2.

36. "It is most proper for anyone associating with others to adapt himself to their habits in his association with them. . . . And so it was most proper for Christ to behave like the rest of men in the matter of food and drink." (*Sum. Theol.*, iii, q. 40, a. 2.)

37. *Sum. contra Gent.*, lib. i, cap. 93.

38. And it may be even said, in a sense, of His divine humility: "There is another feature inflaming the soul to the love of God, that is the divine humility. . . . For Almighty God subjects Himself to each single Angel and every holy soul exactly as though He were the purchased slave of each, whereas in truth He is their very God. To make this known, in His passage, He will minister to them, saying in Psalm lxxxi: *I have said, You are gods.* . . ." Now such humility derives from the multitude of His goodness and divine nobility, as a tree is bowed down by a multitude of fruits. . . ." (*Opusc. de Beatitudine, St. Thomas adscriptum*, cap. ii.)

39. The truth is that the division of the arts into the arts of the beautiful (the Fine Arts) and the useful, however important it may be in other respects, is not what Logicians term an "essential"

E

division; it derives from the end pursued, and the same art can quite well pursue usefulness and beauty at the same time. Such, *par excellence,* is the case with architecture.

40. *Sum. Theol.,* i–ii, q. 57, a. 3, *ad* 3.

41. John of St. Thomas, *Cursus Theol.* (t. vi.), q. 62, disp. 16, a. 4.

42. It is interesting to observe that, by the time of Leonardo da Vinci, the reason for this classification and the position thereby assigned to Painting had ceased to be understood. Leonardo never mentions it without the liveliest indignation: "Painting rightly complains of not being reckoned among the liberal arts, for she is a true daughter of Nature and works through the eye, the noblest of our senses." (*Textes Choisis, Paris,* 1907, § 355.) Leonardo often recurs to this question, treating its *per accidens* with a remarkably sophistic zeal and bitterly inveighing against poets, insisting that their art is far inferior to the painters' because poetry represents with words and for the ear, whereas painting represents for the eye and, "by true likenesses." "Take a poet who describes the beauty of a lady to her lover and a painter who represents her, and you will see to which nature guides the en- amoured critic" (*Ibid.,* § 368; J. P. Richter's Translation, No. 654, in *Leonardo da Vinci,* Sampson Low, London, 1883).—Sculpture, on the other hand, "is not a science, but a mechanical art pro- ducing sweat and bodily fatigue in the practitioner . . ." "The proof that it is so," he goes on to say, "is that the sculptor uses the force of his arms to do his work, beating and shaping the marble or other hard stone whence the figure, which is as it were imprisoned, is to emerge—an entirely mechanical labour which keeps him in a lather of perspiration, smothers him in dust and débris and makes his face pasty and covered with marble dust, like a baker's man covered with flour. He becomes marked all over with splinters and looks as though he were covered with snow- flakes, and his dwelling is dirty, filled with rubbish and dust from the stone. It is quite the opposite for the painter, if the bio- graphies of famous artists are to be trusted. He sits at his ease in front of his work, well clad and holding a light brush dipped in delicate colours. He is as well dressed as he pleases, his dwelling is full of charming panels and beautiful; he often has himself accompanied by music or the reading of various beautiful works, which are listened to with great pleasure, no noise of a hammer or any din interrupting them." (*Ibid.,* § 379.)

In Leonardo's day, then, the "artist" considered himself in a different class from the artisan, and was beginning to look down on him. But, whereas the painter was already an "artist," the sculptor had remained an artisan: although he, too, was rapidly to attain the dignity of "artist." In establishing definitively the Royal Academy of Painting and Sculpture, Colbert was to record and consecrate officially the results of this development.

The word "artist," it may be observed in passing, has had a most chequered career. An *artist* or *artisan* was first of all a *master of arts* (one skilled in the "liberal" or learned arts, including philosophy): ". . . when Pantagruel and Panurge came into the hall, all the school boys, Professors of Arts, Senior-Sophisters, and Batchelors began to clap their hands, as their scurvic custom is." (Rabelais, *Pantagruel*, ii, c. 18, Urquhart's Translation, 1653–96.)

"In good sooth I deny
    That jurists or decretists
    Are more wise than artists."

(*Farce de Guillerme*, Anc. Théâtre français, ii, p. 239.) [The *N.E.D.* (s.v.) quotes (1592) Chettle, Kind-Harts Dr. (1841) 7. *Idiots that think themselves artists because they can English an obligation.*]

Those whom we now call *artists* were then called *artisans*:

"The very cunning artisans
    Inspire with their tools
    Brass, marble, and copper."
        (J. du Bellay, *Les deux Marguerites*.)

"Painter, poet or other artisan."
                    (Montaigne, iii, 25.)

The word "artist" later becomes synonymous with artisan: "Artisan or Artist, artifex, opifex" is the definition in Nicot's *Dictionary*: "one practising or cultivating an art, a scientific man." "What all good workmen and artists in this art (of distillation) set before their minds" (Paré, xxvi, 4). A worker in the great art (sc. alchemy) or again in magic is called an artist: the *Dictionary of the French Academy*, in the edition of 1694, mentions that the word "is used with special reference to such as engage in magical operations." [In English about the same time it had come to mean a professor of magic arts or occult sciences, astrologer or alchemist, later a chemist. (Cf. Milton (1667), *P.L.*, ii. 288: *The Moon whose Orb through Optic Glass the Tuscan Artist views.*")] Only in the 1762 edition of the *Academy Dictionary* does the word appear in its contemporary meaning as distinct from the word "artisan": the divorce between the Fine Arts and the crafts was then complete even in the language.

This divorce was a consequence of the changes which had taken place in the fabric of society and in particular of the rising of the *bourgeoisie*.

43. The artisan is bound by a *commission*, and it is by turning into account the conditions, limitations and hindrances which commissions impose to make his work successful that he best displays the excellence of his art. The modern artist, on the other hand, seems to regard the limiting conditions imposed by the commission as a sacrilegious attempt on his *freedom* as a maker of beauty. Such incapacity to meet the definite requirements of a work to be done in reality denotes in the artist a weakness of the Art itself considered in its generic reason: but it also appears as a price to be paid for the tyrannical and transcendental exigencies of the Beauty which the artist has conceived in his heart. It is therefore a remarkable indication of the kind of conflict mentioned later (pp. 33 and 46) between the "reason" of Art and the "reason of Beauty in the Fine Arts. The artist needs a quite extraordinary energy to achieve perfect harmony between these two formal elements, one of which depends on the material world and the other on the metaphysical or spiritual world. From this point of view it looks as though modern art, since its divorce from the crafts, is tending in its own way to assert the same claim to absolute independence, to *aseity*, as modern philosophy.

44. "That holy man," it is related by Cassian of St. Anthony, "uttered these superhuman and celestical words concerning prayer: *There can be no perfect prayer if the religious is himself aware that he is praying.* (Cassian, Coll., ix, cap. 31.)

45. In Greece, in the heyday of classical art, it was reason alone which kept art in temperance and an admirable harmony. From a comparison of the conditions governing art at Athens with those prevailing in the twelfth and thirteenth centuries some idea can be obtained of the difference between "natural" and "infused" temperance.

46. *Sum. Theol.*, i. q. 5, a. 4, *ad* 1. St. Thomas here intends to give a definition only *per effectum*. When he describes the three elements of the beautiful, he gives a definition which is *essential*.

47. "It is of the nature of the beautiful that the appetite is allayed by the sight or knowledge of it." (*Sum. Theol.*, i–ii, q. 27, a. 1, *ad* 3.)

48. *Ibid.*

49. *Sum. Theol.*, i, q. 39, a. 8. "For beauty three things are requisite. In the first place, intregity or perfection, for whatsoever things are imperfect, by that very fact are ugly; and due proportion or consonance; and again effulgence: so bright coloured objects are said to be beautiful."

50. St. Thomas, *Comment. in lib. de Divin. Nomin, lect.* 6.

51. St. Thomas, *Comment. in Psalm.* Ps. xxv. 5.

52. *De Vera Religione, cap.* 41.

53. *Opusc. de Pulchro et Bono*, attributed to Albertus Magnus and sometimes to St. Thomas. Plotinus (Enneades, i, 6, 2.) discussing beauty in bodies, describes it as "a quality perceived at the first impression: the soul picks it up as it were consciously, recognises and welcomes it, and in a manner accommodates itself to it." He goes on to say that "every formless thing destined to receive shape and form (μορφὴν καὶ εἶδος δέχεσθαι) is ugly and outside the divine reason, so long as it persists without an allotment of such reason or form (ἄμοιρον ὂν λόγου καὶ εἴδους), and this is the essence of ugliness (καὶ τὸ πάντη αἰσχρὸν τοῦτο)," and further on (3) in this important chapter on Beauty "the simple beauty of a colour is caused by a form triumphing over what is obscure in matter (κρατήσει τοῦ ἐν ὕλῃ σκοτεινοῦ), and the presence of an incorporal light which is reason and form (παρουσίᾳ φωτὸς ἀσωμάτου καὶ λόγου καὶ εἴδους ὄντος)."

54. *Sight and hearing* IN THE SERVICE OF REASON, *Sum. Theol.*, i–ii, q. 27, a. 1, *ad* 3.
Sense itself enjoys whatsoever is suitably proportioned only because it is in itself measure and proportion, and so finds therein a likeness to its own nature. "Sense derives pleasure from things duly proportioned, as being similar to itself, for sense too is a

kind of reason, like every cognitive virtue." (*Sum. Theol.* i, q. 5, a. 4, *ad* 1.) On the expression "*a kind of reason*" (*ratio quaedom*, ἡ δ'αἴσθησις ὁ λόγος) cf. Comm. in *de Anima*, lib. 3, lect. 2.

It is permissible to imagine that in glorified bodies all the sense intellectualised, may be of use in the perception of beauty. (Cf. *Sum. Theol.*, iii, Supp., 1. 82, a. 3 and 4.) Even now we are taught by the poets to anticipate in a way such a condition. Baudelaire made the sense of smell a branch of æsthetics.

55. The question of the perception of the beautiful by the mind using the senses as instruments deserves a profound investigation which, in my opinion, has too rarely tempted the subtlety of philosophers. Kant gave it his attention in the *Critique of Judgement*. Unfortunately the direct interesting, and occasionally profound, observations much more frequently met with in that *Critique* than in the other two are vitiated and distorted by his mania for systems and harmony, and above all by the fundamental errors and the subjectivism of his theory of knowledge.

One definition he gives of the beautiful calls for an attentive examination. "The beautiful," says Kant, "is what gives pleasure universally *without a concept*."[1] Such a definition, taken by itself, runs the risk of causing the essential relation of which beauty informs the intelligence to be forgotten. So in the case of Schopenhauer and his disciples it blossomed into an anti-intellectualist apotheosis of Music. Nevertheless, it recalls in its way the much more exact expression of St. Thomas, *id quod visum placet*, what gives pleasure *being seen*, that is to say *being the object of an intuition*. By virtue of this last definition, the perception of the beautiful is not, as the school of Leibniz-Wolff would have it, a confused *conception* of the perception of the thing or of its conformity with an ideal type. (Cf. *Critique of Judgement*, "Analysis of the Beautiful," § xv.)

However usual it may be, because of the nature of the mind, for the perception of the beautiful to be accompanied by the presence or the rough outline of a concept, however confused, and to suggest ideas,[2] nevertheless, that is not its formal constituent:

[1] A concept for Kant is a form imposed by the judgement upon the sensible *datum*, establishing this *datum* either as an object of knowledge or as an object of voluntary appetition.

[2] Cf. on this point some remarkable observations by Baudelaire, in *L' Art Romantique* (Calmann-Lévy's Edition, vol. iii, pp. 213 et seq.). With reference to the *reveries* evoked in him by the Overture to *Lohengrin* which startlingly coincided with those which the same piece had evoked in Liszt,

the splendour or radiance of form glittering in the beautiful thing is not presented to the mind by a concept or an idea, but precisely by the sensible object, intuitively apprehended and having transmitted to it, as it were by an instrumental cause, this radiance of a form. So one may say—it is, in my opinion, the only possible meaning to give to the words used by St. Thomas— that in the perception of the beautiful the mind is, *by means of the intuition of the senses, itself* confronted with a glittering intelligibility (derived, like every intelligibility, in the last analysis from the first intelligibility of the divine Ideas), which by the very fact that it produces the joy of the beautiful cannot be detached or separated from its matrix of the senses and consequently fails to procure an intellectual knowledge susceptible in practice of expression in a concept. Contemplating the object in the intuition which sense has of it, the mind enjoys a presence, enjoys the radiant presence of an intelligibility which does not reveal itself to its eyes as it is. If it turn away from sense to abstract and reason it turns away from its own joy and loses contact with that radiance. To understand this, we must conceive that it is mind and sense combined, or, to use such an expression, the *intellectualised sense* which gives rise to æsthetic joy in the heart. It is thereby clear that the mind has no thought—unless secondarily and reflexively —of abstracting from the sensible particular, in the contemplation of which it is fixed, the intelligible reason for its joy: it is also clear how the beautiful can be such a marvellous *tonic* for the mind without developing in the least its power of abstraction or reasoning, and that the perception of the beautiful is accompanied by that curious feeling of intellectual fullness through which we seem to be swollen with a superior knowledge of the object contemplated though it leaves us powerless to express and possess it by our ideas or make it the object of scientific analysis. So music perhaps more than any other art gives us an enjoyment of being, but does not give us *knowledge* of being; and it would be absurd to make music a substitute for metaphysics. So artistic contemplation affects the heart with a joy which is *before all intellectual*, and it must be admitted with Aristotle (*Poetics*, ix, 3, 1451 b 6) that "poetry is something more philosophic and of graver import than history, since its statements are of the nature rather of universals, whereas those of history are singulars" (Bywater's Translation: Aristotle, *On the Art of*

---

as with the suggestions in the programme drawn up by Wagner of which the poet was ignorant, he points out that "true music suggests similar ideas to different brains." [Whether "true music" is "expressive" and ideological music in the Wagnerian sense is quite another question.]

Poetry, Oxford, 1909), and yet the apprehension of the universal or the intelligible takes place there without speech or any effort of abstraction.[1]

This seizure of an intelligible reality immediately "sensible to the heart," without resorting to the concept as a formal means, creates, upon an entirely different plane and by an entirely different psychological process, a remote analogy between the æsthetic emotion and the mystic graces.

I would add that if the act of perception of the beautiful takes place without speech or any effort of abstraction, the conceptual discourse can nevertheless play an immense part in the *preparation* for that act. Indeed, like the virtue of art itself, taste, or the capacity to perceive beauty and pronounce a judgement on it, presupposes an innate gift, but can be developed by education and instruction, chiefly by the study and rational explanation of works of art. All things being equal, the better informed the mind is of the rules, the methods and the difficulties of art, and above all of the end pursued by the artist and his intentions, the better it is *prepared* to receive by means of the intuition of the senses the intelligible splendour emanating from the work and so spontaneously to perceive and *relish* its beauty. The artist's friends therefore, who know what the artist wanted to do—as the Angels know the Ideals of the Creator—derive far greater enjoyment from his works than the public, and the beauty of some works is a hidden beauty, accessible only to the few.

The eye and the ear are said to accustom themselves to new relations. It is rather the mind which accepts them, as soon as it has realised to what end and to what kind of beauty they are ordered, and so prepares itself to enjoy more fully the work involving them.

So we see what part concepts play in the perception of the beautiful: a part of *disposition*, completely *material*. I have said that this perception is always accompanied by the presence or the rough outline of a concept, however confused. In the simplest case, the extreme case, it might be merely the bare concept of "beautiful," for the mind, being capable of a return upon itself because of its spirituality, knows (at any rate confusedly and *in acuto exercito*) that it is enjoying itself when it is. In fact there is often a whole host of conceptual outlines which the mind is

---

[1] The capital error in Benedetto's Croce's neo-Hegelian æsthetics (Croce, too, is a victim of modern subjectivism: " Beauty is not inherent in things . . .") is the failure to perceive that artistic contemplation, however *intuitive* it may be, is none the less above all *intellectual*. Æsthetics ought to be *intellectualist* and *intuitivist* at the same time.

stimulated to evoke by the fact of its being exercised, and which accompany its intuitive joy, and are dumb. After the first shock when the tongue can find nothing to say, these may be able to break out in exclamations: "What strength! Such solidity!" etc. Contrariwise at times a single word, a concept deposited in the mind ("You think he's a great painter? Taste is his strongest point") will be sufficient to blast in anticipation and prevent the enjoyment one would in the ordinary course have felt before some work of art. But, in all that, the part which concepts play does not go beyond the sphere of dispositive causality.

Again it may be observed that Kant is right in considering *emotion* ("the excitement of vital energies") as a *posterior* and *consecutive* fact in the perception of the beautiful (*ibid.*, § ix). But the first and essential fact for him is the "æsthetic judgement" (in his system its value is wholly subjective); for us it is the intuitive joy of the mind and but secondarily of the senses. To speak less concisely and with greater precision—for joy is essentially an act of the appetitive faculty: *it is of the nature of the beautiful that the appetite is allayed by the sight or knowledge of it* —it is the satisfaction of our faculty of Desire reposing in the proper good of the cognitive faculty perfectly and harmoniously exercised by the intuition of the beautiful. (Cf. *Sum. Theol.*, i–ii, q. 11, a. 1, *ad* 2. *The perfection and the end of any other faculty contained in the object of the appetitive faculty, like a particular in a general*). The beautiful goes straight to the heart: it is a ray of intelligibility attaining it undeviatingly and sometimes bringing tears to the eyes. And this joy is doubtless a "feeling" (*gaudium* in the "intellective appetite" or will, joy properly so called, in which "we have communion with the angels," *ibid.*, q. 31, a. 4, *ad* 3). Nevertheless there it is a question of a very special feeling, *depending simply upon knowledge*, and the happy fullness procured to the mind by a sensible intuition. Emotion in the ordinary meaning of the word, the development of passions and feelings other than this intellectual joy, is merely a result—an absolutely normal result—of that joy: it is as such posterior, if not in time, at all events in the nature of things, to the perception of the beautiful, and remains extrinsic to what formally constitutes the beautiful.

It is interesting to observe that the subjectivist "poison"[1] introduced into modern thought by Kant has almost fatally compelled philosophers to seek for the essence of æsthetic perception, in spite of Kant himself, in emotion. So Kantian

[1] Cf. P. Mattiussi, *Il Veneno kantiano*.

subjectivism has borne its latest fruit in the *Einfühlung* theory of Lipps and Volkelt, which brings the perception of the beautiful back to a projection or infusion of our emotions and feelings into the object (cf. M. de Wulf, *L'Œuvre d'art et la beauté*, "Annals of the Philosophical Institute of Louvain," vol. iv, 1920, pp. 421 et seq.).

56. "Beauty is a certain kind of good" (Cajetan, in i–ii, q. 27, a. 1). So the Greeks combined both notions in one word καλοκἀγαθία, synonymous for Eudemus with ἠθικὴ ἀρετή.

The beautiful, we have seen, is in direct relation to the faculty of knowing. It is by definition essential for it to procure a certain intuitive delight of the mind (and, in our case, of the senses). But if the happy exercise of a faculty, e.g. the mind, causes the metaphysical well-being and, as it were, the blossoming of that faculty, so satisfying the *natural appetite* which makes one with its essence, this bloom of the act nevertheless is properly *pleasure, joy* or *delight*, only because it is immediately gathered by the subject's own appetitive faculty, the *appetitus elicitus* which there finds its goal and haven of repose.[1] For according to the text of St. Thomas quoted in the last note "the end and perfection of every other faculty are contained in the object of the appetitive faculty as the particular is enclosed in the general." (*Sum Theol.*, i–ii, q. 11, a. 1, *ad* 2). The beautiful therefore is in an essential and necessary, albeit indirect, relation with the appetite. For this reason it is "a kind of good" and ought to be considered, as is said in the text, as "essentially delightful." The function of beauty is to gratify desire in the mind, the faculty of enjoyment in the faculty of knowing.

The texts of St. Thomas on this point of doctrine need to be carefully constructed. He first wrote in the *Commentary upon the Sentences:* "Beauty has not the nature of an object of appetite except so far as it assumes the nature of good; then it becomes truly an object of appetite. But of its own nature it has effulgence." (In *I Sent.*, d. 31, q. 2, a. 1, *ad* 4.) And again: "To say that the ends of appetite are the good, tranquillity, and the beautiful,

---

[1] Angels enjoy beauty because they possess intelligence and will. A being impossibly possessing intelligence only would still be able to perceive beauty *in its roots* and objective conditions, but not in the delight through which alone it succeeds in establishing itself. To give delight in knowledge is not only a property of beauty (as Gredt, *Metaph. gen.*, I, c. 2, § 5, insists) but a formal constituent of it. (It is the fact of stirring desire and awakening love which is a *propria passio* of the beautiful.) I do not therefore agree with Gredt, still less with de Munnynck, who gives *placet* in "quod visum placet" a wholly empirical and sensualist interpretation. (Cf. note 63*b infra*).

is not to say that the ends are various. For by the very fact of a thing desiring food, it desires at the same time what is beautiful and tranquillity; the beautiful indeed so far as it is in itself specified and modified by its inclusion in the nature of the good: the good, however, adds the nature of the perfect to other things. Hence whoever desires the good, by the very fact desires also the beautiful. Now tranquillity involves the removal of disturbances and hindrances, for by the very fact that a thing is desired, the removal of whatever obstacles to it there may be is also desired. So that in the one desire, good is desired, and the beautiful, and tranquillity" (*De Ver.*, q. 22, a. 1, *ad* 12; Commentary on the Maxim of Denys in Chap. IV of the Divine Attributes: *pulchrum omnia appetunt*).

Here are two texts of first importance from the *Summa Theologica:* "The beautiful and the good are the same as regards the subject: they have the same foundation, namely form, and the good is therefore commended as beautiful. But they differ in concept. For the good, strictly speaking, regards the appetite, that being good which all things desire; and therefore it partakes of the nature of an end, for the appetite is as it were a sort of movement to the thing. The beautiful, however, concerns the force of knowledge, for things are said to be beautiful when they give pleasure at sight. Therefore beauty consists in proper proportion, because the sense derives pleasure from things properly proportioned, as being similar to itself, for sense also is a kind of reason (λόγος τις) like every cognitive virtue: and as knowledge comes about through assimilation, and similitude is concerned with form, the beautiful strictly pertains to the concept of a formal cause." (*Sum. Theol.* i, q. 5, a. 4, *ad* 1.)

"The beautiful is the same thing as the good, differing only conceptually. That being good which all things desire, it is of the nature of good that the appetite is allayed by it: but *it is of the nature of the beautiful that the appetite is allayed by the sight or knowledge of it* . . . and so it is clear that the beautiful adds over and above the good a certain order to the force of knowledge. So let that be termed good which simply gratifies the appetite: *but let that be termed beautiful the mere apprehension of which gives pleasure.*" (*Sum. Theol.*, i–ii, q. 27, a. 1, *ad* 3.)

To make these texts agree, it must first be observed that the beautiful can be related to the appetite in two ways: either as subsumed in the specific concept of the good and as the object of an elicit desire (we like and desire a thing because it is beautiful); or as being a special good delighting the appetitive faculty in the faculty of knowledge and satisfying the latter's natural desire (we say that a thing is beautiful because the sight of it gives us pleasure). In the first case the coincidence of the beautiful and the good is merely material (*re seu subjecto*): in the second, on the other hand, the bare concept of it implies that it is the special good in question.

The text from the *Sentences* must be considered under the first head: the beautiful is desirable only in so far as it assumes the aspect of the good (that is to say, generally speaking, of an object the possession of which strikes the subject as good and towards which it directs its desire). On that score truth also is desirable in the same way, and such desirability is not implicit in the concept of the true or the beautiful, although it is an immediate property of the beautiful. Under the second head, however, it is of the essence of the beautiful to procure that special good which is delight in knowledge: this is implicit in its bare concept and for that reason there is no parity between the beautiful and the true.

So in the next from the *De Veritate* it is a question of the good considered as such and, unlike the beautiful, defined by the perfection it brings to the subject. There is then a material coincidence of the good and the beautiful, but a conceptual difference (as in the case of the true and the good)—which does not prevent the beautiful, because it perfects the faculty of knowledge as object of delight, from including on that account, in its bare concept, a relation to the appetite.

As for the two capital texts from the *Summa*, the first shows clearly that if the beautiful differs (*ratione*) from the good in that it does not directly confront the appetite, and belongs by itself to the domain of formal causality, nevertheless it has in its definition of giving pleasure by being seen, and implies also of necessity, a relation to the appetite. The second text teaches as precisely as could be desired that such a relation to the appetite as the object the simple apprehension of which gives pleasure is of the very concept of the beautiful. So that beauty, while directly confronting the faculty of knowledge, indirectly concerns, by its very essence, the appetitive faculty, as was said above. *It is of the nature of the beautiful that the appetite is allayed by the sight or knowledge of it.*

57. Denys the Areopagite, *De Divin. Nomin.*, cap. iv; St. Thomas, lect. 9. I shall continue to call the philosopher *the Aeropagite*, from his age-old possession of the title. Modern critics call him *the pseudo-Denys*.

58. "Her have I loved, and have sought her out from my youth, and have desired to take her for my spouse, and I became *a lover of her beauty*" (*Wisdom*, viii, 2).

59. *De Divin. Nomin.*, cap. 4; St. Thomas, lect. 10.

60. It should be observed that the conditions of the beautiful are much more strictly determined in nature than in art, the end of natural beings and the formal brilliance which can shine in them being themselves much more strictly determined than those of works of art. In nature, for instance, there certainly is a perfect type (whether we know it or not) of the proportions of the male or female body, because the natural end of the human organism is a thing fixed and invariably determined. But the beauty of a work of art *not being the beauty of the object represented*, Painting and Sculpture are in no way bound to the determination and imitation of any particular type. The art of pagan antiquity deemed itself so bound merely because of an extrinsic condition, because it represented above all the gods of an anthropomorphic religion.

60*b*. Τὸν θεοειδῆ νοῦν ἐπιλάμποντα (Plotinus, *Enneades*, i, 6, c. 5, 16).

61. Cf. Lamennais, *De l'Art et du Beau*, chap. ii.

62. "Beauty, health and such-like are predicated in a way with respect to something: because a certain suitable mixture of humours produces health in a lad, but not in an old man, and what is health for a lion may mean death for a man. Health, therefore, is a proportion of humours in relation to a particular nature. In like manner beauty (sc. of the body) consists in the proportion of its limbs and colours, and so the beauty of one differs from the beauty of another" (St. Thomas, *Comment. in Psalm.*, Ps. xliv. 2).

63. St. Thomas, *Comment. in lib. de Divin. Nomin.*, cap. iv, lect. 5. Eugène Delacroix from his painter's point of view made some very just observations in an article published in the *Revue des Deux Mondes*, July, 15, 1857, on the "Variations du Beau" (cf. *Œuvres littéraires*, vol. i, *Études esthétiques*, Paris, Crès, 1923, pp. 37 et seq.). Philosophising on the question with more acumen than many professional philosophers, he had realised that the multiplicity of the forms of the beautiful did not impair in the least

its objectivity: "I have never said and nobody would dare to say that it can possibly vary in essence, for then it would no longer be the beautiful but mere caprice or fancy. But its character can change; an aspect of beauty which once charmed a far-off civilization no longer surprises or pleases us as much as one in accordance with our feelings or, if you like, our prejudices. *Nunquam in eodem statu permanent*, said ancient Job of man." There is, in different words, a statement of the fundamentally *analogical* character of the idea of beauty (cf. "Projet d'article sur le beau," *ibid.*, pp. 141 et seq.).

"Beauty must be seen where the artist has chosen to put it," said Delacroix again ("Questions sur le beau," *Revue des Deux Mondes*, July 15, 1854; *ibid.*, p. 32); and as early as his Diary (end of 1823 and beginning of 1824): "A Greek and an Englishman are each of them beautiful in his own way, which has nothing in common with the other" (*Journal*, Plon, 1893, vol. i, p. 47).

63*b*. In an essay published in 1923 ("L'Esthétique de Saint Thomas" in *S. Tommaso d'Aquino*, Publ. della Fac. di Filos. del' Univ. del Sacro Cuore, Milan, Vita e Pensiero), Fr. de Munnynck endeavoured to cast doubt on this point, thereby taking the *quod visum placet* and the Scholastic theory of the beautiful quite materially (cf. Fr. Wébert's review in *Bulletin thomiste*, January, 1925). The classic table of transcendentals (*ens, res, unum, aliquid, verum, bonum*) does not exhaust all transcendental values, and if the beautiful is not included, the reason is that it can be reduced to one of them (to the good; the beautiful being that which in things confronts the minds as the object of pleasure in an intuition). St. Thomas constantly affirms that the beautiful and the good, metaphysically, are the same thing in reality and differ only conceptually (*Pulchrum et bonum sunt idem subjecto, sola ratione differunt*, i, q. 5, a. 4, *ad* 1). It is so with all the transcendentals, which are identical in the object but differ in concepts. For this reason *quicumque appetit bonum, appetit ex hoc ipso pulchrum* (*De Verit.*, q. 22, a. 1, *ad* 12). If it is true that *pulchrum est idem bono, sola ratione differens* (i–ii, q. 27, a. 1, *ad* 3), why should the beautiful not be a transcendental as well as the good? It is in fact the splendour of all the transcendentals together. Wherever there is something existing there are being, form, and proportion; and whenever there are being, form and proportion, there is some beauty. Beauty is in the things of sense, it is also and *par excellence* in the things of the spirit. The honourable good has a spiritual beauty, a thing is said to be honourable (*honestum*) when it possesses some excellent quality worthy of honour because of its spiritual beauty" (ii–ii, q. 145, a. 3). Beauty is found in the contemplative life essentially and by itself: "Beauty consists in a kind of effulgence and proper proportion. . . . In the contemplative life, which consists in the exercise of reason, beauty is found by itself essentially" (*ibid.*, q. 180, a. 2, *ad* 3). Beauty is properly (*formaliter eminenter*) attributed to God, like being, unity and goodness. "The reason why the (divine) Beauty is in so many ways the cause of all things," teaches St. Thomas (Comment. in *Nom. Divin.*, c. iv, lect. 5.), "is because the good and the beautiful are the same; because all things desire the beautiful and the good, as cause, in every way; and because there is nothing but has some share in the beautiful and the good, every single thing being beautiful and good according to its own form." In the same way Beauty is appropriated to the Word (*Sum. Theol.*, i, q. 39, a. 8).

The property of causing joy, of "giving pleasure," implicit in the idea of the beautiful is itself, it should be remembered, transcendental and analogical, and not to be referred, without making great nonsense of it, to pleasure of the senses alone or the "enjoyable good" considered as opposed to the other kinds of good. *Honesta etiam sunt delectabilia*, observes St. Thomas (*Sum. Theol.*, i. q. 5, a. 6, obj. 2; and ii–ii, q. 145, a. 3). *Honestum est naturaliter homini delectabile. . . . Omne utile et honestum, est aliqualiter delectabile, sed non conventitur.* And is not the effect of virtue to make difficult things pleasing? Is there not a supreme spiritual pleasure in contemplation? Is not God the supreme archetype of all that dispenses joy? *Intra in gaudium Domini tui.* It is because the pleasure implied by the beautiful is transcendental and analogous, that the diversity of kinds of such pleasure and the forms of beauty in no way prevents the objectivity of such beauty. Such diversity springs from the metaphysical analogy, not from a psychological "relativity" in the modern meaning of the word (cf. note 63).

64. *Analoga analogata* of an analogous concept (*analogum analogans*) are the various things in which such a concept is realised and which it suits.

65. In God alone all these perfections become identified according to their formal reason: in Him Truth is Beauty, Goodness, Unity, and they are He. In the things of this world, on the other hand, truth, beauty, goodness, etc., are aspects of being *distinct according to their formal reason* and what is *true simpliciter*

(speaking absolutely) may be *good* or *beautiful* only *secundum quid* (in a certain relation . . . what is *beautiful simpliciter may* be *good* or *true* only *secundum quid. . . .* For this reason beauty, truth and goodness (moral good) command distinct spheres of human activity, and it would be foolish to deny *a priori* that they may possibly conflict, on the pretext that transcendentals are indissolubly bound to one another. As a principle of metaphysics this is perfectly true, but it needs to be properly understood.

66. *De Divinis Nominibus*, cap iv; lessons 5 and 6 of the Commentary of St. Thomas.

67. St. Thomas, *ibid.*, lect. 5.

68. *Sum. Theol.*, i, q. 39, a. 8.

69. St. Augustine, *De Doctr. Christ.*, i, 5.

70. Baudelaire, *L'Art romantique*. Baudelaire is here reproducing an extract from the preface to his own translation, *Nouvelles Histoires Extraordinaires*, an extract inspired by and almost a translation of a passage in a lecture by Poe, *The Poetic Principle:* "We have still a thirst unquenchable. . . . This thirst belongs to the immortality of Man. It is at once a consequence and an indication of his perennial existence. It is the desire of the moth for the star. It is no mere appreciation of the Beauty before us, but a wild effort to reach the Beauty above. Inspired by an ecstatic prescience of the glories beyond the grave, we struggle by multiform combinations among the things and thoughts of Time to attain a portion of that Loveliness whose very elements perhaps appertain to eternity alone. And thus when by Poetry, or when by Music, the most entrancing of the Poetic moods, we find ourselves melted into tears, we weep them not, as the Abbate Gravina supposes, through excess of pleasure, but through a certain petulant, impatient sorrow at our inability to grasp *now*, wholly here on earth, at once and for ever, those divine and rapturous joys of which *through* the poem, or *through* the music, we attain to but brief and indeterminate glimpses.
"The struggle to apprehend the supernal Loveliness—this struggle, on the part of souls fittingly constituted—has given to the world all that which it (the world) has ever been enabled at once to understand and to *feel* as poetic" (cf. Edgar Allan Poe's *Tales and Poems*, vol. iv, London, J. C. Nimmo, 1884, at pp. 205–6).

71. Denys the Areopagite, *De Divin. Nomin.*, cap. iv (St. Thomas, lect. 4).

72. Opusc. lxviii, *in libr. Boetii de Hebdom.*, princ.

73. *Prov.*, viii, 31.

74. *Metaph.*, lib. i, c. 2, 982 b.

75. Ruysbrock (*Vie de Rusbrock*, preface to the selected works published by Hello, p. lii).

76. Charles Maurras, *L'Avenir de l'Intelligence.*

77. The name Technique may be given to the whole collection of these rules; but on condition of amplifying considerably and elevating the ordinary meaning of the word "technique." For it is a question not of material processes only, but also, and chiefly of the ways and means of proceeding in the intellectual sphere which the artist uses to attain the end of his art. Such ways are determined, like paths laid out before through a tangled thicket. But they have to be discovered. And the most elevated of them, those most closely approximating to the individuality of the work spiritually conceived by the artist, are strictly personal to him and discoverable by one individual only.

78. "It is clear," writes Baudelaire, "that systems of rhetoric and prosodies are not forms of tyranny arbitrarily devised, but a collection of rules required by the very organisation of the spiritual being: prosodies and systems of rhetoric have never prevented originality from manifesting itself distinctly. The opposite would be far more true, that they have assisted the development of originality."
And again: "It would be quite a new departure in the history of the arts for a critic to turn poet, a reversal of every psychic law, a monstrosity: on the other hand, every great poet becomes naturally, fatally, a critic. I am sorry for poets who are guided by instinct alone; I consider them incomplete. A crisis inevitably arises in the spiritual life of all great poets, when they try to discover the reason of their art, to ascertain the obscure laws by virtue of which they have produced, and to derive from such a scrutiny a set of rules whose divine object is infallibility in poetic production. It would be a prodigy for a critic to turn poet and it is an impossibility for a poet not to have in him at the same time the stuff of a critic" (*L'Art romantique*).

79. A remark of the painter David.

80. Cf. the very title which Descartes at first thought of giving
to the treatise to which the *Discourse on Method* is the preface:
"*Project of a Universal Science capable of raising our nature to its
highest degree of perfection*, with in addition Dioptrics Meteorics
and Geometry, wherein the most curious matters which the Author
has been able to select as evidence of the universal science he
proposes are treated *in such a way that even those who have never
been to School can understand them.*" Some years later—doubtless
in 1641—Descartes was working at a dialogue in French which
he left unfinished with the title: "The Quest of Truth by the light
of Nature, which, unsullied and *without enlisting the aid either of
Religion or Philosophy*, determines the opinions an honest man
should hold *touching everything that can occupy his mind, and
penetrates the innermost secrets of the most curious sciences.*"

81. "So that the mind shall be free from the labour of thinking
things out clearly itself and yet all things nevertheless turn out
correctly" (Gerh., *Phil.*, vii).

82. *Sum. Theol.*, i–ii, q. 51, a. 1.

83. The Royal academy of Painting and Sculpture, as is well
known, was definitively established in 1663.
I would here mention A. Vaillant's *Théorie de l'Architecture*
(Paris, 1919). On the subject of academicism, as on the generic
notion of art, the author's thesis, although informed by a rigid but
rather narrow-minded positivism, happily coincides with the
doctrine of the Schoolmen. "It was in the reign of Louis XIV,"
writes M. Vaillant, "that the teaching of the Fine Arts began to
assume the scholastic character which we now know. . . . It
must be admitted that academic influence was very great, but
not as yet in any degree harmful: the reason was that the empirical
methods of the Masters of apprenticeship and their ancient
customs remained in full vigour down to the suppression of the
Guilds. As they declined, so the effect of their teaching dim-
inished: for doctrine, which is the soul of art, was naturally
contained in the traditions, in the manner in which the artist
received and assimilated the commission and responded to
it. . . ."
"As long as apprenticeship continued to be the means of forming artists and artisans, no necessity for any general theory was
felt. Architects, in particular, had a system which was main-

tained by the example of and intimate collaboration with the professional life of the master, as Étienne Boileau's *Livre des Métiers* clearly shows. When teaching was put in the place of the living and very varied action of the master, a grave error was committed."

"The academic breach with the *daubers of painting* and the *marble cutters and polishers* produced no advantage to art or the artist: it deprived the workman of healthy contact with what was above him and supremely good. Academicians also ceased to be independent and lost along with technique the rational organisation of working at art."

One consequence of the rupture was the disappearance of the technique of crushing colours. Artists lost in course of time the feeling for the chemical reactions to which colours and colouring materials are subject when mixed, the nature of the binding, and how to apply it. "Van Eyck's pictures, five centuries old, are as fresh to-day as they ever were. Can modern pictures," asks M. Vaillant, "hope for such a protracted youth?" "How leaden modern painting is becoming!" replies M. Jacques Blanche, with reference to Monet. "In a few years now the most glowing picture becomes desiccated and is ruined. We admire ruins, ruins dating from yesterday. You can have no idea what *le Linge* was like when it first appeared! I should think I ought to blame myself or bewail the state of my eyes, if I had not been a witness, during the last five years, of the destruction of a master-piece, Delacroix's *Trajan*, in the Gallery at Rouen. I have seen it become tarnished and crack: now it is a mere brown smudge . . ." (Jacques-Émile Blanche, *Propos de peintre, de David à Degas*, Paris, 1919).

Augustin Cochin also writes: "Academic teaching, created" [or rather erected into a unique and universal law] "by the Encyclopædists, from Diderot to Condorcet, has killed popular art in one generation, a phenomenon which is perhaps unique in history. Teaching in school instead of forming in the studio, making pupils learn instead of making them do,—explaining instead of pointing out and correcting—is what constitutes the reformation conceived by the philosophers and imposed by the Revolution. Isolated artists have survived, but like rocks battered by the sea of banality and ignorance, not like great trees in the forest" ("Les Sociétés de pensée," in the *Correspondant* of February 10, 1920).

84. "After these [sc. the painters after the Romans, who always imitated each other so that their art constantly declined

from age to age] came Giotto: he was a Florentine and born in the lonely mountains where only goats and such beasts dwell, but feeling the aspect of nature to resemble art, he began by drawing on the rocks the movements of the goats he kept. And he went on to draw all the animals which were to be found in the country, in such wise that after much study he excelled not only the masters of his time but all those of many bygone ages . . ." (Leonardo da Vinci, *Textes choisis*, published by Péladan, Paris 1907).

85. This point is well expressed by Goethe's verses in *Wilhelm Meisters Wanderjahre*:

> "Zu erfinden, zu beschliessen
>   Bleibe Kunstler oft allein," . . . etc.

translated as follows by Thomas Carlyle:

> "While inventing and effecting,
>   Artist, by thyself continue long:
> The result art thou expecting,
>   Haste and see it in the throng.
> Here in others look, discover
>   What thy own life's course has been:
> And thy deeds of years past over.
>   In thy fellow man be seen."

(Cf. *Wilhelm Meister's Apprenticeship and Travels*, vol. ii, p. 329, London, Chapman & Hall, 1899.)

86. Man cannot dispense with a master. But in the anarchy which characterises the modern world, the power of the master, being unacknowledged, has merely become less profitable to the pupil and tyrannical.

"As everyone to-day wants to be king, nobody knows how to govern himself," wrote Baudelaire. "Now that everyone is left to his own devices, a master to-day has many unknown pupils for whom he is not responsible, and his power, being underground and involuntary, ranges far beyond his studio into regions where his doctrine cannot be understood" (*Curiosités esthétiques*, Salon of 1846).

87. Cf. *Sum. Theol.*, i, q. 117, a. 1; *ibid.*, *ad* 1 and *ad* 3.

88. Cf. note 64.

89. These rules, which it is the province of the various systems to define, are unchangeable only when considered *formally* and *analogically*.

"In æsthetics there is never any fundamental innovation. The laws of beauty are eternal, the most violent innovations obey them unawares: they obey them in their own way and that is the point of interest" (Max Jacob, *Art Poétique*, Paris, 1922).

90. It follows that the philosopher and the critic are competent and ought to judge the value of artistic schools, as well as their truth or falsity, the good or bad influence of their principles, but that considerations of the sort are utterly insufficient to judge the poet or the artist himself. It is of cardinal importance to distinguish here whether it is an *artist* or a *poet* who is under consideration, a man who really has the virtue of Art, a *practical* and *operative*, not a speculative, virtue. If his system is false, a philosopher is of no account, for in that case he cannot *tell the truth*, unless by accident: if his system is false, an artist can be of some account, of very great account, because he can *create beauty* in spite of the system and in spite of the inferiority of the form of art which is his. From the point of view of the work done there is more artistic truth (and so more genuine "classic") in a romantic with the habit than in a classic without it. When we speak of an artist or a poet we should always be careful not to miss the virtue which may be in either, not to offend something naturally sacred.

90b. On the question of progress in general, more especially progress in art, cf. the author's *Theonas*, chapters vii, viii, and ix.

91. Cf. pp. 15, 16.

92. In i–ii, q. 57, a. 5, *ad* 3.

93. The *conception* of the work is entirely different from the mere choice of subject; the subject is simply the *matter* of the conception, and an artist or a poet can even derive certain advantages—as is very well explained by Goethe—from having such matter supplied from elsewhere. It is also entirely different from an abstract *idea*, an intellectual theme or thesis an artist might have in mind. Goethe was once asked what idea he wanted to express in *Tasso*. "What idea?" said he. "How can I possibly tell? I had Tasso's life, I had my own life . . . But don't go and think that everything would be lost, if there were no idea,

no abstract thought to be discovered behind a work. You come and ask me what idea I have endeavoured to embody in my Faust ! As if I knew, as if I myself could tell ! *From Heaven, through Earth, down to Hell*, there's an explanation, if you want one: but that is not the idea, that's the *development of the action . . .*" (*Conversations with Eckermann*, May 6, 1827.)

Nor is the conception of the work the plan of the work or its scheme of construction (which is already a realisation—in the mind). It is a simple view, although virtually very rich in multiplicity, of the work to be done apprehended in its individual soul, a view which is as it were a spiritual germ or *seminal reason* of the work, closely related to what M. Bergson calls *intuition* or *dynamic schema*, concerning not only the intelligence but also the imagination and the sensibility of the artist, answering a certain unique shade of emotion and sympathy, and therefore inexpressible in concepts. What painters call their "vision" of things plays an essential part therein.

Such a conception of the work, depending on the whole spiritual and sensitive being of the artist and above all on the correctitude of his appetite in regard to Beauty, and bearing on the *end* of the activity, may be described in relation to Art as the intention of the ends of the moral virtues in relation to Prudence. It belongs to a different order from the *means*, the *ways* of realisation, which are the peculiar province of the virtue of Art, as the means of attaining the ends of the moral virtues are the peculiar province of the virtue of Prudence. And it is, in every particular case, the fixed point to which the artist orders the means which Art puts in his possession.

M. Blanche tells us that "the means are *everything* in painting" (*De David à Degas*, p. 151). Let there be no misunderstanding. The means are the peculiar province of the artistic habit and in this sense the dictum may be accepted. But means exist only in relation to an end, and the means which "are everything" would be *nothing* themselves without the conception or the vision which they tend to realise and from which the whole activity of the artist depends.

Clearly the more exalted the conception, the more the means run the risk of proving inadequate. Is not Cézanne an eminent example of such an inadequacy of the means in relation to the elevation of the conception ? If he is so great and exercises such a dominating influence over contemporary art, it is because he introduced a conception or a vision of superior quality—*his little sensation* as he used to say—which his means were inadequate to express. Hence his complaints at his incapacity *to realise*: "Don't you see, Monsieur Vollard, the outline keeps escaping me !"—and his touching regret at "not being Bouguereau," who, at any rate, did "*realise*" and "developed his personality."

94. Ὁποῖός ποθ' ἕκαστός ἐστι, τοιοῦτο καὶ τὸ τέλος φαίνεται αὐτῷ (Aristotle, *Eth. Nic.*, lib. iii, c. 7, 1114 a 32. Cf. St. Thomas, *Commentary*, lect. 13; *Sum. Theol.*, i, q. 83, a. 1, *ad* 5). In teaching (*Sum. Theol.*, i–ii, q. 58, a. 5, *ad* 2) that "the principles of artificial objects are not distinguished by us as good or bad *according to the disposition of our appetite*, like *ends* which are the principles of moral acts, but solely on consideration of their nature," St. Thomas has in mind the *moral* dispositions of the appetite on the one hand (cf. Cajetan, *loc. cit.*) and, on the other, art considered according as "objects of production are not related to art as first principles, but only as material" (*ibid.*, q. 65, a. 1, *ad* 4). This is not the case with the Fine Arts (ends indeed are principles in the practical order, and the work to be done in the Fine Arts has all the dignity of a true *end*).

95. St. Augustine, *De Moribus Ecclesiae*, cap. 15. *Virtus est ordo amoris.*

96. Quoted by M. Étienne Charles in the *Renaissance de l'Art français*, April 1918.

97. Louise Clermont, *Émile Clermont, sa vie, son œuvre*, Grasset, 1919.

98. In so far as Apollinism reigns supreme in Greek art. It would, however, be interesting to discover if a Dionysiac art did not continue to lurk in the shadow, such as that to which Goethe seems to allude in the Second Part of *Faust* with the Phorcides and the Cabeiri stirring in the Classical Walpurgis Night.

99. "Reason is the first principle of all human work." (St. Thomas, *Sum. Theol.*, i–ii, q. 58, a. 2.)
I would here record the remarkable testimony of Eugène Delacroix: "Art, then, is not what the vulgar think, that is to say a kind of inspiration coming from nobody knows where, proceeding at haphazard and presenting only the picturesque surface of things. *It is reason itself embellished by genius, but a necessary course and confined by superior laws.* This brings me back to the difference between Mozart and Beethoven. 'Where

Beethoven is obscure,' Chopin said to me, 'and seems to be lacking in unity, it is not a rather wild attempt at originality, considered to be to his credit, which is the cause, but he is turning his back on eternal principles: now Mozart never does that'" (Delacroix's *Journal*, April 7, 1849).

It goes without saying that the pre-eminence of true inspiration, concerning which we may say with Aristotle that it would be improper for one moved by a superior principle to listen to the counsels of human reason, is not therefore denied. Reason is the first principle of all human work—reason alone where human work within man's capacity is concerned, reason exalted by an instinct of divine origin where human work controlled by a higher law is concerned (of the natural order as regards art and speculation, of the supernatural in the case of prophecy or the gifts of the Holy Ghost). I would add that as the devil is the ape of God, so it is aping genuine inspiration, which is above reason, to seek for the law governing the work (and not merely certain more or less valuable materials) in dreams or the whole organic night below the level of reason.

100. Baudelaire again says: "Construction, the framework, so to speak, is the surest guarantee of the mysterious life of the works of the mind" (*Notes nouvelles sur Edgar Poe*, the preface to the translation, *Nouv. Hist. extraord.*). "Everything that is beautiful and noble is the result of reason and calculation" (*l'Art Romantique*). And again: "Music gives the idea of space. So does every art, more or less; for the arts are *number* and number is a translation of space" (*Mon cœur mis à nu*).

Nevertheless, the relation of the Arts to Logic is much deeper and much more universal still than their relation to the science of Number.

100b. From this point of view there is much to be gained from the ideas of M. Le Corbusier, and the comparisons drawn by him between the art of the architect and that of the engineer ("A house is a machine to be lived in"). It would be a mistake, however, to think that everything must be reduced under pain of sin to what performs a useful function: that would be falling into a kind of Jansenist æsthetic. If certain mechanical constructions (a motor-car, steamship, truck, or aeroplane) are beautiful once their type is definitely fixed, and every part strictly conceived in accordance with its use in the whole, the reason is that the law of utility here covers and embodies a more profound law, the law of mathematical harmony, and more generally of logic.

It is logic which gives the useful its æsthetic value, and logic overflows the useful. In nature there is a multitude of characteristics of an entirely ornamental kind and of no practical utility. The pattern on the wing of a butterfly is of no *practical use*, but everything in it is *logically necessary* (in relation to a certain idea gratuitously chosen).

Delacroix observed that in the great architect there is "an absolutely essential harmony of great good sense and great inspiration. The details of utility which are the starting-point of architecture, details which are of the essence, take precedence of every sort of ornament. The architect, nevertheless, is an artist only in so far as he decorates the *useful* elements appropriately: they are his theme. I say *appropriately*, for even after establishing the exact relation in every particular of his plan with the practical uses to which it will be put, he can only decorate his plan in a certain way. He is not at liberty to lavish or curtail decorations. They must be as suited to the plan, as the plan has been made to suit its practical uses" (*Journal*, June 14, 1850). It is in this sense that M. Auguste Perret is fond of repeating that Fénelon wrote the best treatise on architecture in the following passage from his *Speech to the Academy*: "No part of a building should be there merely as a decoration: the architect, aiming always at beautiful proportions, should rather make decorative every part necesssary for supporting a building."

101. Cf. Maurice Denis, *Les Nouvelles Directions de l'Art chrétien* ("Nouvelles Théories," Rouart et Watelin, 1922): "Any sort of lying is intolerable in the temple of Truth."

102. Paul Gsell, *Rodin.*

103. *Le Symbolisme et l'Art religieux moderne (op. cit.).*

104. John of St. Thomas, *Curs. Theol.*, t. vi., q. 62, disp. 16, a. 4.

105. The Parthenon, as is well known, is not geometrically regular. It obeys a very much higher logic and regularity, the zenithal direction of its pillars and the curve of its horizontal lines and its floors making up for the apparent distortions of line and plan in visual perception, and thereby assuring perhaps greater stability against the seismic oscillation of the soil of Attica.

106. *Vide supra*, p 15.

107. John of St. Thomas, *ibid.*

108. Architecture also provides remarkable examples of the primacy accorded by the art of the Middle Ages to the *intellectual and spiritual* construction of the work at the expense of material correctness, in regard to which the technical equipment and the theoretical knowledge of the old builders were inadequate. In the architecture of the Middle Ages "Geometrical correctness or anything approaching it is nowhere to be found; there is never a rectilinear alignment, never a right-angled crossing or symmetrical counterpart—irregularities and after-thoughts everywhere. The centring for the vault had to be specially prepared for each bay, even in the best-constructed buildings of mediæval art. The curves, especially in the ribs of the vaulting, are no more accurate than the alignment and the division of the bays. No more is the symmetry of their equilibrium. Keystones are not found in the middle of the arches or the vaulting—and sometimes the displacement is serious. . . . The right side of a building is hardly ever symmetrical with the left. . . . Everything is approximate in an art which is, nevertheless, very deliberate, but careless of exactitude. It may be that the sincerity and ingenuousness of such architecture owe their permanence of charm to this simplicity of construction" (A. Vaillant, *op. cit.*, pp. 119, 364). The same writer also draws attention to the fact that as it was impossible to make building plans on paper as nowadays and the only drawing-paper available was rare and costly parchment, sparingly used and washed for service again, "the projected work was conceived in its essential details chiefly by means of a reduced model. The builders began to worry about details only at the moment when they were about to take shape, when the scale was exactly known and they could use familiar rules and elements. The solution of every building problem was considered and discovered and difficulties overcome on the *dump* where the work was done. The same thing applies to workmen nowadays, with this difference that they are devoid of education and have never served an apprenticeship, so that their experience is a mere rough rule of thumb."

"Considering the enormous quantity of paper which we find necessary to plan and prepare the erection of our modern buildings, the calculations indispensable to the achievement of our slightest projects, we may stand amazed at the high intellectual power, the range of memory, and the positive talent, of the masters of works and foremen builders of those times, who had the skill to build such grandiose and magnificent monuments, inventing daily and ceaselessly perfecting. The power displayed in the art of the Middle Ages is extraordinary, in spite of its fumbling and scanty technical knowledge."

The lack of skill in the primitive painters is not due to the inadequacy of their material means only. It is also due to what may be called in their case a kind of *intellectualist realism.* "Their clumsiness," writes Maurice Denis, "consists in painting objects according to their habitual knowledge of them, instead of painting them, like the moderns, according to a preconceived idea of the picturesque or the æsthetic. The Primitive . . . prefers reality to the appearance of reality. Rather than resign himself to the distortions of perspective which have no interest for his maiden eye, *he makes the picture of things conform to the idea he has of them*" (*Théories*, Paris, Rouart et Watelin). I would say that his eye is dominated entirely by a sort of *rational instinct.*

109. These *stultae questiones* are such as, if raised in any science or discipline, would run contrary to the first conditions implied by that very science or discipline. (Cf. St. Thomas, *Comment. in Ep. ad Titum*, iii, 9. The reference is to St. Paul's exhortation: *avoid foolish questions, and genealogies, and contentions, and strivings about the law; for they are unprofitable and vain.*)

109b. Too many theories have reduced us to a state of exasperation at the mention of the word "classic": it is so hackneyed. Nevertheless definitions of words are free. The important thing is to distinguish the authentic from the fake—they sometimes bear the same label—and to realise all the liberty the former requires.

Gino Severini, as is well known, published in 1921 a significant book entitled *Du Cubisme au Classicisme* (Paris, Povolozky), in which he invited the protractor, the compass and number to provide the means of escaping from mere expediency and good taste. Science and technique, which are included in the still material means of art, are, to be sure, not *sufficient* conditions, and it would be a great mistake to expect everything from them. But they are the first *necessary* conditions of honest art, and Severini's book is a most valuable testimony to this fact.

110. Jean Cocteau, *Le Coq et l'Arlequin.*

111. *Republic*, book x.

112. "We have too long accustomed ourselves to consider truth in art from the one point of view of imitation. There is no paradox in maintaining the opposite, that make-believe is synonymous with lying, and lying with the intention of deceiving. A painting conforms to its own truth, to truth itself, when it says well what it has to say and fulfils its decorative rôle" (Maurice Denis, *loc. cit.*).

"What a mistake it is to think that drawing means accuracy ! Drawing means the will to create a form: the more powerful and reasoned the will, the more beautiful the drawing. And that's all there is to it: the merit of the best Primitives lies not in their simplicity, as people keep on saying, but in their concern for the whole, which is merely drawing. The best Cubists are like them" (Max Jacob, *Art poétique*, Paris, 1922). I notice an interesting equivalent of the Thomist definition of Art, *recta ratio factibilium*, in the following definition by the same poet: "Art is the will to exteriorise oneself by selected means" (Preface to *Cornet à dés*). What he then goes on to call "placing," and rightly distinguishes from "art" or "style," depends on the spiritual quality of the work. "Once he has *placed* his work, the author can employ every means of charming—language, rhythm, music and wit. When a singer has his voice well placed he can amuse himself with trills." I would add that if a philosophical work is "*placed*," the author may perhaps be permitted to employ the special charm to be found in the barbarism of technical terms.

113. *Poet.*, iv, 1448 b 5–14.

114. Or, more probably, from the desire to signify an object by means of an ideogram, with perhaps a magical intention: for such drawings, being necessarily in the dark, could not have been made to be looked at. In a general way—as appears from a study of the vases recently discovered at Susa, and dating, no doubt, from about 3000 B.C.—the art of drawing would seem to have begun by being a writing and by fulfilling hieroglyphic, ideographic, or even heraldic needs, absolutely devoid of æstheticism, concern for beauty being introduced only much later.

115. *Poet.*, i, 1447 a 28.

116. "[Cézanne] once asked me what collectors thought of Rosa Bonheur. I told him it was generally agreed that the *Laboureur Nivernais* was stunning.—'Yes,' replied Cézanne,

'*it's horribly like* the real thing'" (Ambroise Vollard, *Paul Cézanne*, Paris, Cres, 1919).

116*b*. In some articles which appeared in the *Nord-Sud* (cf. more particularly June–July 1917, October 1917, March 1918), Paul Reverdy asserted in the clearest possible way the claims of a *purely creative* æsthetic, free from all concern with evocation or imitation—claims which constituted the deep interest of the Cubist movement, but far exceeded it, inasmuch as they displayed to an impossible degree one of the extreme exigencies of art.

I hope that my exposition may have made it sufficiently clear that the evocation or imitation of things is in no way the *object* of art, but that our art nevertheless cannot recompose its peculiar world, its autonomous "poetic reality," without first of all distinguishing, in whatever is, the forms it manifests, and so *resembling* things in a more profound and mysterious manner than any direct evocation possibly can.

"The image," writes Reverdy, "is a pure creation of the mind. It cannot emerge from a comparision but only from the bringing together of two more or less distant realities. . . . An image is not striking because it is *brutal* or *fantastic*—but because the association of ideas is remote and exact. . . . No image is produced by comparing (always inadequately) two disproportionate realities. A striking image, on the contrary, one new to the mind, is produced by bringing into relation without comparision two distant realities whose relations *the mind alone* has seized."

This passage must be kept in mind, if modern poetry and poetry in general are to be understood. The image so conceived is the opposite of *metaphor*, which compares one known thing with another known thing the better to express the former by covering it with the latter. It *discovers* one thing with the help of another, and by their resemblance makes the unknown known. In a more general way I have already observed elsewhere (*Petite Logique*, No. 20) "the most striking and unforeseen images used by the poets may perhaps owe their origin to the difficulties man experiences when he wants to tell himself and make himself really *see* the commonest things with the help of the imagery of language, difficulties which compel him to renew that imagery" (cf. J. Paulhan, *Jacob Cow, ou si les mots sont des signes*).

Words are symbols no less than resounding matter; we use them in speech in place of things which cannot be made to appear themselves in our midst (Aristotle, 1 *Elench.*, 1); that is the reason why, in the youth of language, words were pregnant with such a terrible, magical and magnificent power. The powerfully metaphysical instinct of primitive man might go astray in particular applications; it still bore witness to the symbolic nature and to that astounding mystery bestowed upon the human race, of being able *to give* things *names*. But words are not pure symbols ("formal symbols"), they are imperfect symbols which become quickly loaded with subjectivity, each dragging after it the whole psychological stuff of a race. In particular a prolonged social use tends of itself to make them lose their spirituality, their symbolic nature, to change them into *things* of value in themselves, letting off mental reactions without the intervention of any meaning; the less intervention in fact, the more reaction. Many instructive observations on this point are to be found in Jean Paulhan's *Expérience du Proverbe*.

The besetting sin of such a writer as Hugo is staking all upon the material dynamism of the word-*thing*. I think on the contrary that it is the province of the poet, who uses words as the material of his work, to react against this tendency of the symbol to transform itself into a thing and so to maintain or recover by force, in the sensitive flesh of the word, the spirituality of language. Hence an invention, a creation of fresh images, which may appear obscure but is nevertheless imposed by absolute precision. Modern poetry, with a courage which is sometimes ridiculous, has undertaken to scour language. In spite of contradictory appearances and stray phenomena, like Dadaism some years ago and "free" words, it is making rather towards objectivity, trying to find a form of expression which will not convey a lie, but in which the mind will force the word with its whole weight of matter to be faithfully significant in the cloistered world of the poem.

116c. Lecturing one day at the Academy of Painting on Poussin's *Eliezer and Rebecca*, Philippe de Champagne expressed regret that the Master had not seen fit to depict "the camels mentioned in Holy Writ." Lebrun thereupon replied that "M. Poussin, in a constant endeavour to purify and disencumber the subject of his paintings and to portray attractively the main action he was dealing with, had rejected every uncouth object likely to debauch the eye of the spectator and amuse him with trivial details." Alas ! the facile descent to the undignified and the commonplace was to prove only too easy: and of Poussin himself, "that philosophic painter," Delacroix could say "that perhaps he was only so called because he devoted to the idea a little more than painting requires" ("Variations du Beau," *Revue des Deux*

Mondes, July 15, 1857; *Œuvres Littéraires,* i, "Études esthétiques").[1] Nevertheless the advice in itself was sound.[2]

Cf. the following passage from Nietzsche on style: "How is *decadence in literature* characterised ? By the fact that in it life no longer animates the whole. Words become predominant and leap right out of the sentence to which they belong, the sentences themselves trespass beyond their bounds, and obscure the sense of the whole page, and the page in its turn gains in vigour at the cost of the whole,—the whole is no longer a whole. But this is the formula for every *decadent* style: there is always anarchy among the atoms, disaggregation of the will—in moral terms 'freedom of the individual,' extended into a political theory: 'equal rights for all.' Life, *equal* vitality, all the vitality and exuberance of life driven back into the smallest structure, and the remainder left almost lifeless. Everywhere paralysis, distress and numbness, or hostility and chaos: both striking one with ever-increasing force as one ascends higher in the forms of organisation. The whole no longer lives at all: it is composed, reckoned up, artificial, a fictitious thing."

"Victor Hugo and Richard Wagner," wrote Nietzsche again, "they both prove one and the same thing: that in declining civilisations, wherever the mob is allowed to decide, genuineness becomes superfluous, prejudicial, unfavourable. The actor, alone, can still kindle *great* enthusiasm. And thus it is his *golden age* which is now dawning—his and that of all those who are in any way related to him. With drums and fifes, Wagner marches at the head of all artists in declamation, in display and virtuosity. . . ." (Nietzsche, *The Case of Wagner,* translated by A. M. Ludovici, George Allen & Unwin, London, 1911).

"The works of Hugo," wrote Delacroix in 1844, "are like the rough copy of a man of talent: he says everything that comes into his head" (Delacroix's *Journal,* September 22, 1844).

[1] Cf. in the *Journal,* s.d. June 6, 1851, the suggestive parallel between Poussin and Lesueur, and the very proper praise of the latter.

[2] It may also have been ill suited to the case which Philippe de Champagne had in mind, for in the narrative in Genesis the camels play a part which is not simply accessory or picturesque, but essential to the main action. "And when he had made the camels lie down without the town near a well of water in the evening, at the time when women are wont to come out to draw water, he said: O Lord the God of my master Abraham, meet me to-day, I beseech Thee, and show kindness to my master Abraham. Behold, I stand nigh the spring of water, and the daughters of the inhabitants of this city will come out to draw water. Now, therefore, the maid to whom I shall say, Let down thy pitcher that I may drink: and she shall answer, Drink, and I will give thy camels drink also: let it be the same whom Thou hast provided for Thy servant Isaac, and by this I shall understand, that Thou hast showed kindness to my master " (*Genesis* xxiv. 11-14.)

117. *Jeremias*, i, 6.

It might be said that, without being a form of knowledge and precisely because it is not a form of knowledge, art makes up for the deficiencies in our direct intellectual knowledge of the particular, which is the privilege of the angelic mind. It expresses the particular not in a mental word or concept, but in the material work it makes. And by the way of the senses it leads the creative mind of the artist to an obscure experimental perception—incapable of speculative expression, of individual realities apprehended as such in the bosom of the universe itself. "For a child," Max Jacob once said, "an individual stands alone in a species; for a man, he is taken into consideration; for an artist, he is left out of consideration."

118. St. Thomas, *Comment. in Psalm.* Prolog.

119. The delight of the sense itself is required merely *ministerialiter*; that is why the artist towers so high above it and is so free to discipline it: nevertheless it is required.

120. It is because of these laws, that, according to Baudelaire's remark, "seen at too great a distance to analyse or even to understand its subject, a picture by Delacroix has already moved the soul to a rich emotion of happiness or melancholy" (*Curiosités esthétiques*, Salon of 1885). Elsewhere (ibid., Salon of 1846) Baudelaire wrote: "The good way of determining whether a picture is harmonious is to consider it from far enough off to understand neither the subject nor the lines. If it is harmonious, it already has a meaning, it has already taken its place in the repertory of memories."

121. The truth is, it is difficult to determine in what precisely this imitation-copy consists, the concept of which seems so clear to minds which have their being among the simplified schemata of the popular imagination.

Is it the imitation or the copy of what the thing in itself *is* and its intelligible *type*? But that is an object of conception, not of sensation, a thing invisible and intangible, which art, consequently, cannot directly reproduce. Is it the imitation or the copy of the *sensations* produced in us by the thing? But the sensations attain the consciousness of each one of us only as refracted by an inner atmosphere of memories and emotions, and are, moreover, eternally changing in a flux in which all things become distorted and are continually intermingled, so that from the point of view of *pure sensation* it must be admitted with the Futurists that "a galloping horse has not four hoofs but twenty, that our bodies sink into the sofas on which we sit and the sofas sink into us, that the motor-'bus rushes into the houses it goes past, and that the houses in turn hurl themselves upon the motor- 'bus and become one with it. . . ."

The reproduction or exact copy of nature thus appears as the object of an impossible pursuit—a concept which vanishes when an attempt is made to define it. In practice it resolves itself into the idea of such a representation of things as photography or casting would give, or rather—for such mechanical processes themselves produce results which are "false" as far as our perception is concerned—into the idea of a representation of things *capable of giving us an illusion and deceiving our senses* (it is then no longer a copy pure and simple but presupposes, on the contrary, an artificial faking); in short, into that naturalist make-believe which concerns only the art of the Musée Grévin or Madame Tussaud's.

122. Cf. Louis Dimier, *Histoire de la peinture française au XIXᵉ siècle*, Paris, Delagrave.

123. Ambroise Vollard, *Paul Cézanne*, Paris, Crès, 1919. "On Nature," that is to say, contemplating and deriving inspiration from Nature. If it were to be understood as doing Poussin over again *by painting according to nature, with nature for a constituent feature*, Cézanne's observation would deserve all the criticism it has received. "It is not by sensation you become classical, but by the mind" (Gino Severini, *Du Cubisme au Classicisme*). Cf. G. Severini, *Cézanne et le Cézannisme*, "L'Esprit Nouveau," Nos. 11, 12, and 13, 1921; Émile Bernard, "La Méthode de Paul Cézanne," *Mercure de France*, March 1, 1920); "L'erreur de Cézanne," *ibid.*, May 1, 1926.

The very proper definition suggested by Maurice Denis over thirty years ago is well known: "It must be borne in mind that before becoming some anecdote or other, a picture is essentially a plane surface covered with colours grouped in a certain order" (*Art et Critique*, August 23, 1890).

"One should not paint from Nature," said that most scrupulous observer of Nature, Edgar Degas (recorded by J. E. Blanche, *De David à Degas*).

"In fact," observes Baudelaire, "all good and genuine draughts- men draw according to the picture inscribed in their brains, and not according to Nature. If the admirable sketches of Raphael,

F

Watteau and a hundred others are urged against this statement, I would answer: they are indeed very detailed notes, but simply notes. When a real artist comes down to the definitive execution of his work, the model will be rather a *nuisance* to him than a help. It even happens that men like Daumier and M. Guys, long practised in exercising their memories and filling them with pictures, find their main faculty upset and well-nigh paralysed when confronted with the model and the multiplicity of details it involves. A duel then takes place between the will to see everything, to forget nothing, and the faculty of memory, which has acquired the habit of quickly absorbing the general colour, the silhouette and the arabesque of the outline. An artist with a perfect feeling for form, but accustomed to exercise chiefly his memory and imagination, then finds himself, harassed as it were, by a pack of details, all clamouring for fair treatment with the frenzy of a mob in a passion for absolute equality. Any kind of fair treatment is then of necessity outraged, all harmony ruined and sacrificed; trivialities assume gigantic, meannesses tyrannical, proportions. The further the artist goes towards an impartial treatment of detail, the more the anarchy increases. Whether he be long- or short-sighted, all hierarchy and subordination vanish" (*L'Art romantique*).

124. "The artist, on the contrary, *sees*: that is to say," Rodin felicitously explained, "*his eye grafted on his heart* reads deep down into the bosom of Nature" (*Rodin*, Entretiens réunis par Paul Gsell, Paris, Grasset, 1911).

125. Baudelaire, *Curiosités esthétiques*, Le Musée Bonne-Nouvelle.
The observations advanced in the text make it possible to reconcile two series of apparently contradictory expressions current amongst artists.
Thoughtful and conscientious artists such as Gauguin and Maurice Denis—and a hundred others in contemporary painting—will tell you for example that "what is most of all to be deplored" is "this notion that Art consists in *copying* something" (*Théories*). "To think that Art consists in *copying* or reproducing things exactly is to pervert the meaning of Art" (*ibid.*). "Copying" is here understood in the proper sense of the word, imitation materially considered with make-believe for its object.
Ingres, on the other hand, or Rodin, more impassioned and not so acutely intelligent, will tell you that "you must go and *copy, copy* like a fool, slavishly *copy* what you find under your

eyes" (Amaury-Duval, *L'Atelier d'Ingres*). "Obey Nature in all things and never try to give her orders. My one ambition is to be slavishly faithful to Nature" (Paul Gsell, *Rodin*). The words "copying" and "slavishly" are here understood in a most improper sense: in reality it is not a question of slavishly imitating the object, but, what is entirely different, of manifesting with the utmost fidelity, at the cost of every "distortion" which may be necessary, the *form* or ray of intelligibility the brilliance of which is apprehended in the real. Ingres, as Maurice Denis judiciously points out (*Théories*), meant to copy the Beauty *which he perceived in Nature through frequenting the Greeks and Raphael*:[1] he "thought he would make us copy Nature," says Amaury-Duval, "by making us copy it as he saw it," and he was the first, in Odilon Redon's phrase, "to turn out monsters," Rodin, on the other hand, only attacked (and how justly !) those who pretended to "embellish" or "idealise" Nature according to æsthetic formulæ, to portray it "not as it is, but as it ought to be," and he had to admit that he *emphasised, accentuated, and exaggerated* in order to reproduce not only "the exterior" but "the spirit as well, which, certainly, is also part of Nature,"—the spirit, another word to describe what is here called "form."

It must, however, be observed that the "distortions" produced by the painter or the sculptor are in most cases rather the quite spontaneous result of a personal "vision" than the effect of deliberate calculation. By a phenomenon which psychologists could easily explain, they simply and honestly believe themselves to be copying Nature, whereas in fact they are expressing in matter a secret which Nature has communicated to their souls. "If I have changed anything in Nature," said Rodin, "it was unconsciously on the spot. The feeling influencing my vision showed me Nature just as I copied it. . . . If I had wanted to modify what I saw and embellish it, I should have produced nothing of any value." For this reason "it may be said that every innovator

[1] It was therefore not only a " form " naïvely apprehended in the real, but also an artificial "ideal" unconsciously impregnating his mind and vision, that Ingres was trying to manifest. This explains why Baudelaire, judging the artist's intention from the work, attributed to Ingres principles utterly different from those the painter professed: " I shall be understood by everyone who has compared the different methods the principal masters have of drawing, when I say that the drawing of Ingres is the drawing of a man with a system. He thinks that Nature ought to be corrected and amended: that successful, pleasing trickery, perpetrated to gratify the eye, is not only a right, but a duty. Hitherto it had been maintained that Nature ought to be interpreted and translated as a whole with all its logic: but in the works of the master in question there is often deceit, guile, violence, sometimes cheating and tripping-up " (*Curiosités esthétiques*).

since Cimabue," possessed with the same anxiety to interpret
more faithfully, also "believed that he was submitting himself
to Nature" (J. E. Blanche, *Propos de Peintre, de David à Degas*).

So in order to imitate, the artist transforms, as Toppfer said—
a genial, gossiping forerunner whose *Menus propos* contains
many judicious observations on the subject—but without being
himself aware, as a rule, that he is transforming. This in some
ways not unnatural illusion, this disparity between what the
artist is doing and what he thinks he is doing, may perhaps
explain the remarkable difference to be observed between the
great art of the Græco-Latin classics, so filially free in regard to
Nature and their theory, occasionally so flatly naturalist (e.g.
the story of the grapes of Zeuxis). Not that such a theory, it must
be admitted, does not prevent their art, if it relaxes its efforts in the
slightest degree, from being seriously threatened by naturalism.
From Greek idealism, which claims to copy an ideal type of
Nature, the transition, happily observed by the author of *Théories*,
to naturalism which copies Nature itself in its contingent mater-
iality is very simple indeed. So make-believe *dates back to
antiquity*, as Jacques Blanche says, but to the decadent period of
ancient art.

If mediæval art has been safeguarded in this respect by its
sublime simplicity and humility, and also by the hieratic traditions
which it inherited from the Byzantines, so that it maintains itself
as a general rule on the spiritual level to which the later classic art
only attains as a summit, Renaissance art, on the contrary,
allowed itself to be seriously contaminated.

Is it not strange to hear an artist with so comprehensive
a mind as Leonardo apologising for painting with truly humiliat-
ing arguments: "A painting representing the father of a family
has had the good fortune to be caressed by his grandchildren,
although they were still in long clothes: the dog and the cat of the
household did likewise, and it was a wondrous sight to see." "I
once saw a painting deceive a dog by its likeness to his master and
the animal was overjoyed to see it. I have also seen dogs bark
and eager to bite other dogs in a picture, and a monkey frolic
like anything before the painting of a monkey, and swallows
flying about and alighting upon the painted railings depicted on
the windows of buildings." "A painter paints a picture so that
whoever sees it forthwith yawns; and this happens every time the
eyes rest on that picture, which has been painted with such an
intention" (*Textes Choisis*, published by Péladan, 357, 362, 363).

Thank Heaven Leonardo lived painting otherwise than he
thought it, although with him "the Renaissance æsthetic,

expression by the subject,[1] becomes definitely established," and although it may be truthfully said of him with André Suarès: "He seems to live only for knowledge: much less for creation. . . . So long as he is studying and observing, he is the slave of Nature. Once he begins to invent, he is the slave of his ideas: theory in him stifles the ardent play of creation. Most of his faces, although born of fire, are lukewarm, and some of them as cold as ice."[2]

At all events it was such theories as Leonardo delighted in which, subsequently codified by the teaching of the Academies, have compelled the modern artist to react and become thoughtfully conscious of his creative liberty in regard to Nature ("Nature is simply a dictionary," was a favourite saying of Delacroix), at the expense sometimes of the ingenuousness of his vision, imperilled by calculation and analysis to the greater detriment of his art.

The distinction before indicated (cf. note 93) between the "vision" of the artist or, again, his invention, his *conception* of the work and the *means* of execution or realisation which he employs, cannot in this connection be too strictly insisted upon.

On the side of vision or conception, simplicity, spontaneity, unself-conscious candour, is the most precious gift the artist can have, a unique gift, a gift *par excellence*, considered by Goethe to be "demoniac," so gratuitous does it seem to be and beyond analysis.

If such a gift is superseded by some system or calculation, some prejudice of "style" such as Baudelaire alleged against Ingres or such as can be seen in certain Cubists, the "deformation" or, rather, ingenious *transformation* which owes its simplicity to spiritual fidelity to the *form* shining in things and their profound life, gives way to an artificial "deformation," to *deformation* in the sense of violence or deceit; and art so far withers.

On the side of means, on the other hand, it is reflection, consciousness, and artifice, which are required. Between the conception and the accomplishment of the work there is a great

[1] Maurice Denis, *Théories*. The importance of this very simple principle, often overlooked since the Renaissance, cannot be too strongly insisted upon. It is a *leit-motiv* with Maurice Denis that *expression in art proceeds from the work itself and the means employed, not from the subject represented*. The failure to appreciate this principle, to which the image-makers of old were so spontaneously faithful, and to which their work owed such boldness and nobility at once, is one reason for the chilly decrepitude into which modern religious art has sunk.

[2] *Le Voyage du Condottiere, Vers Venice.*

gap—the peculiar domain of art and its means—filled by an interplay of deliberate combinations which make realisation "the result of patiently elaborated and conscious logic" (Paul Valéry) and an ever-vigilant prudence. So the Venetians artificially substitute for the magic of sunlight "the equivalent magic of colour" (*Théories*), and in our day the transformations which Picasso and his followers make things undergo seem essentially wilfully determined.

If the "distortions" due to the vision or the conception of the artist impose themselves upon him—in the precise degree in which his art is really alive—with a sincere and as it were instinctive spontaneity, there may then be others depending upon the *means* of art, and these are deliberate and calculated.[1] Many instances are to be found in the masters and in the greatest of them all, in Rembrandt, of such transformations, distortions, abbreviations and redispositions, all consciously effected. The works of the Primitives are full of them, because they were more concerned with *symbolising* objects or actions than representing their appearances. In the same order of ideas, Goethe made an engraving by Rubens the occasion of a profitable lesson to the worthy Eckermann (Eckermann, *Conversations with Goethe,* August 18, 1827). Goethe showed the engraving to Eckermann, who proceeded to point out all its beauties.

"'All these objects reproduced here,' Goethe asked, 'the flock of sheep, the haycart, the horses, the labourers returning home, from what side are they lighted?'

"'They are lighted from our side and cast their shadows towards the inside of the picture. The labourers returning home, to begin with, are in full light and that produces a splendid effect . . .'

"'But how has Rubens got that fine effect?'

"'By making the clear figures stand out against a dark background.'

"'But how is that dark background produced?'

"'By the dense shadow cast by the group of trees beside the figures—is it possible?' I added, all taken aback. 'The figures cast their shadows towards the inside of the picture and the group of trees, on the contrary, casts its shadow in our direction! The light comes from two opposite sides! That's something absolutely contrary to Nature.'

---

[1] In such a case the proper expression would perhaps be, as Severin observes, *construction* or *reconstruction* rather than *distortion*: in any event what is here important is the spiritual infallibility of art and not the mere approximation of taste and sensibility.

"'That's just the point,' said Goethe with the trace of a smile. 'That's where Rubens shows himself a master, proving that his free spirit is above Nature and deals with Nature as befits his exalted aim. The double light is certainly doing violence to Nature: you can always say that it is contrary to Nature: but if it is contrary to Nature, I would also add that it is above Nature. I say that it is a bold stroke of the Master, who shows with genius that art is not entirely subject to the necessities imposed by Nature and that it has its peculiar laws. . . . The artist stands in a double relation to Nature: he is at once its master and its slave. He is its slave in the sense that he must use earthly means in order to be understood: he is its master in the sense that he subjects these earthly means and makes them serve his high intentions. The artist wants to address the world by means of a general effect, but he cannot find such a general effect in Nature: it is the fruit of his own mind or, if you like, his mind fertilised by the puff of a divine breath. If we cast only a careless glance on this picture, everything in it strikes us as so Natural that we take it to be a mere copy from Nature. But it is not so. Such a beautiful picture was never seen in Nature, any more than a landscape by Poussin or Claude Lorrain: we think them very natural, but in reality we seek them in vain.'"

126. Cf. *Sum. Theol.*, i, q. 45, a. 8. The capacity of matter to obey the human artist who can make it yield better results than any it could give under the influence of physical agents provides theologians (cf. St. Thomas, *Compendium Theologiae*, cap. 104; Garrigou-Lagrange, *De Revelatione*, vol. i, p. 377) with the most profound analogy to the *obediential faculty* in things and souls with regard to God, which delivers them in the very depth of their being to the invincible power of the first Agent, for His action to raise them to the supernatural order or to miraculous results. "And I went down into the potter's house, and, behold, he was doing a work on the wheel. . . . Then the word of the Lord came to me, saying, Cannot I do with you, as this potter, O house of Israel? saith the Lord. Behold, as clay is in the hand of the potter, so are you in My hand, O house of Israel" (*Jeremias* xviii. 3, 5, 6).

127. Cf. St. Thomas, in *I Sent.*, d. 32, q. 1, 3, 2.

128. The ancient maxim *ars imitatur naturam*, does not mean: "art imitates Nature by *reproducing* it," but "art imitates Nature *by doing or operating* like Nature, *ars imitatur naturam* IN SUA

OPERATIONE." In this sense St. Thomas applies the maxim to Medicine, which is certainly not an "imitative art" (*Sum. Theol.*, i, q. 117, a. 1). [This meaning, too, should be given to Claudel's observation: "Our works and the means we use are not different from nature's" (*Art poétique*).]

129. Paul Claudel, *La Messe là-bas*.—*Sicchè vostr'art a Dio quasi è nipote*, said Dante (*Inf.*, xi, 105), [and cf. Leonardo: *noi* (sc. we painters) *per arte possiamo essere detti nipoti a Dio*.]

130. Quoted by M. Albert André in his recent book on *Renoir* (Crés).

131. From this point of view the *symbolist* conception, as expounded by Maurice Denis, seems to be not yet quite free from some confusion. "Symbolism," according to M. Denis (*Nouvelles Théories*), "is the art of translating and *producing states of soul* by means of relations of colours and forms. These relations are invented or borrowed from Nature and become signs or symbols of such states of soul: they are able to suggest them. . . . The Symbol claims *to produce directly in the soul of the spectator the whole gamut of human emotions* by means of the gamut of colours and forms, that is to say sensations, corresponding to them. . . ." And after quoting the following passage from Bergson: "*The object of art* is to put to sleep the active, or rather resistant, faculties of our personality and so lead us to a state of perfect docility in which we can realise the idea suggested to us, sympathise with the feeling expressed"—Maurice Denis adds: "Once all our confused memories have been so revivified, all our subconscious energies so set going, the work of art worthy of the name creates in us a mystic state, or one at any rate analogous to the mystic vision, and, in a certain degree, makes our hearts sensitive to God."

It is perfectly true that the *effect* of art is to produce emotional states in us, but that is not its *object* or its *end*: a fine distinction, if you like, but still extremely important. Everything goes awry if what is simply a *conjoined effect*, a mere *repercussion*, is to be taken for the *end*, and the *end* itself (the making of a work in which the splendour of a form shines on a proportioned matter) be conceived as a mere *means* (of producing states of soul and emotions in someone else, putting his powers of resistance to sleep and setting his subconsciousness going).

132. Cf. Aristotle, *Polit.*, viii, 7, 1341 b 40; *Poet.*, vi, 1449 b 27.

133. *Lettres de Marie-Charles Dulac*, Bloud, 1905: letter of February 6, 1896.

134. There is no school for teaching "Christian art" in the sense here defined. On the other hand, there may very well be schools for teaching *ecclesiastical* or *sacred* art which, given its peculiar object, has its peculiar conditions—and which also, alas ! is terribly in need of being raised from the decadence into which it has fallen.

I will not discuss this decadence here—there would be too much to say—but quote instead the words of Marie-Charles Dulac: "There is something I should like and for which I pray, that everything beautiful be brought back to God and serve His praise. Everything we see in creatures and creation ought to be turned back to Him; and what distresses me is to see His Spouse, Our Holy Mother the Church, decked out with horrors. Every exterior manifestation of the Church is so ugly and she within so fair. No effort is spared to make her look grotesque. Her body has from the beginning been delivered naked to the beasts; then artists set their souls on decorating her; then vanity and finally commerce take a hand and, so bedizened, she is made an object of ridicule. Here is another sort of beast, not so noble as a lion and more vicious . . ." (Letter of June 25, 1897).

"They are satisfied with work which is dead . . . They are on an ultra-inferior level, so far as the understanding of art is concerned. I am not now speaking of the taste of the public: I have noticed it as early as the time of Michelangelo and Rubens in the Low Countries—for I can see no trace of spiritual life in those fat bodies. You understand that it is not so much bulk I mean, but the utter absence of inner life; and that close after an epoch in which the heart had expanded so freely, had spoken so candidly, there should have been a return to the coarse meat of paganism to end up with the indecencies of Louis XIV.

"But you are aware, what makes the artist is not the artist: it is the people who pray. And people who pray only get what they ask: nowadays it is not even suggested to them that they should try for something more. I firmly believe that there will be some leading lights; for considering the modern Greeks who imitate the atrophied images of long ago, the Protestants who do nothing at all and the Latins who do the first thing that comes into their heads, I really think that the Lord is not served by the manifestation of Beauty, that He is not praised by the Fine Arts at all in proportion to the graces He puts to their credit, and that a sin has been committed in rejecting what was

holy and within our reach and taking what was tarnished"
(Letter of May 13, 1898).

Cf. on the same subject l'Abbé Marraud's Essay: "Imagerie
religieuse et l'art populaire" and Alexander Cingria's "La
Décadence de l'Art Sacré" (*Cahiers Vaudois* edition, Lausanne).

With regard to this book, which he considers to be "the most
thorough and penetrating report" which has appeared "on this
distressing subject," Paul Claudel wrote in an important letter to
Alexander Cingria: "They [sc. the cause of this decadence] may
be summed up in one: the divorce unhappily consummated last
century between the propositions of the Faith and the powers of
imagination and sensibility which are pre-eminently the privilege
of the artist. On the one hand, a certain religious school, chiefly
in France, where the Quietist and Jansenist heresies have succeeded
in a sinister way in exaggerating its nature, has reserved for the
act of adherence to a religion a too violently exclusive part for
the spirit stripped of the flesh—whereas what was baptized and
will rise again at the Last Day is the whole man in the complete
and indissoluble unity of his double nature. On the other hand,
the art subsequent to the Council of Trent (generally known
under the absurd name of Baroque—I have, like yourself, the
liveliest admiration for it, as you well know) seems to have
taken for its object, not the object of Gothic art, the *representation*
of the concrete facts and historical truths of the Faith before the
eyes of the public like a great open Bible, but the *demonstration*
with noise, pomp and eloquence, and often with the most affecting
pathos, of that space, vacant like a medallion, access to which is
forbidden to our ceremoniously dismissed senses. And so we have
saints indicating to us by expression and gesture what is invisible
and inexpressible; we have all the riotous abundance of orna-
mentation, angels in a whir of wings upholding a picture blurred
and concealed by religious ceremonies, statues moved as it were
by a great wind from elsewhere. But before that *elsewhere* the
imagination recoils in terror, becomes discouraged, and devotes
all its resources to displaying the frame whose essential object
is to pay honour to its contents, by methods which are almost
official, degenerating only too quickly into formulæ and clichés."

After remarking that in the nineteenth century the "crisis of
an ill-nurtured imagination" consummated the divorce between
the senses—"which had been diverted from the supernatural
world, without any effort having been made to make it accessible
or desirable to them"—and the theological virtues, Claudel
goes on: "That essential spring of the creator, the Imagination
(or in other words the desire to procure immediately by resources

peculiar to oneself and one's neighbour, with the help of elements assembled together, a certain picture of a world at once delightful, significant and reasonable) is thereby secretly injured, and with it the capacity to take the object seriously."

"As for the Church, by losing the envelope of Art, in the last century it became like a man stripped of his clothes: in other words, that sacred body, composed of men, believers and sinners alike, displayed itself for the first time materially before the eyes of the world in all its nakedness, in a kind of exhibitionism and permanent translation of its wounds and infirmities. To anyone who has the heart to look at them, modern churches are as interesting and pathetic as a heavily-laden confession. Their ugliness is the ostentation to the world of all our sins and short-comings, our weakness, poverty, timidity of faith and feeling, dryness of heart, disgust with the supernatural domination by conventions and formulæ, extravagance of individual disorderly practices, worldly luxury, avarice, boasting, sulkiness, Pharisaism and bombast. But, nevertheless, the soul within remains alive, infinitely suffering, patient and hoping, the soul which may be guessed at in all those poor old women with their absurd and deplorable hats in whose prayers I have for the last thirty years taken part at Low Masses in every church and chapel in the world. . . . Yes, even in such ghastly churches as Notre-Dame-des-Champs or Saint Jean l'Évangéliste in Paris or the basilicas of Lourdes—a more tragic spectacle to anyone who gives them a thought, than the ruins of the Cathedral of Rheims—even there God is present: we can have confidence in Him and He can trust us always to spare Him by our small personal means, in default of worthy thanks, a humiliation as great as that of Bethlehem" (*Revue des Jeunes*, August 25, 1919).

134b. "Art," wrote Léon Bloy in a familiar passage, "is an aboriginal parasite of the skin of the first serpent. Hence derive its overweening pride and power of suggestion. It is self-sufficient like a god, and the flowered crowns of princes, compared with its head-dress of lightning, are like necklaces of paste. It will no more submit to worship than to obedience, and no man's will can make it bow before any altar. It may consent, out of the superfluity of its riches, to give alms to temples and palaces, when it finds there what it wants, but you must not ask it for a thimbleful over and above. . . . There may be exceptionally unhappy souls to be encountered who are at once artists and Christians, but there cannot possibly be a Christian art" (*Belluaires et Porchers*).

Here, as often happens, Bloy goes to the extreme, the better to bring home a profound antinomy. And that this antinomy does in fact make the possibility of a Christian art singularly difficult, even in a spiritually privileged tradition, may be agreed. Nevertheless it is not insoluble, for Nature is not essentially bad, as the Lutherans and the Jansenists thought. However deeply wounded it may be by sin, especially where it is rising up, it can be cured by grace. Or do you think that the grace of Christ is powerless, that it meets an insurmountable obstacle in any one of the things, and the noblest things at that, which proceed from God, that it is incapable of setting art and beauty free, of making them docile to the Spirit of God, *ad obediendum fidei in omnibus gentibus !* God knows no opposite. The mind of man can, and must, be given back to Him. Only a price must be put upon it, a higher price than Christian humanism believed. It is a Manichæan blasphemy to pretend with André Gide that the devil collaborates in every work of art, and an essential absurdity, for evil is not creative. The extravagances of Léon Bloy, needless to say, have quite a different meaning, and merely tend to assert a mysterious dramatic reversal of fortune.

134c. Such divine inspiration in the natural order was expressly admitted by the Ancients, and in particular by the author of the *Eudemian Ethics* in his well-known chapter on Good Fortune (vii, 14). St. Thomas also admits it, distinguishing it from the essentially supernatural inspiration peculiar to the gifts of the Holy Ghost (*Sum. Theol.*, i–ii, q. 68, a. 1 and 2). Cf. the Author's *Réponse à Jean Cocteau*, note 3.

135. I do not mean that in order to do Christian work the artist must be a saint who might be canonised or a mystic who has attained to transforming union. I mean that, strictly speaking, mystic contemplation and sanctity in the artist are the goal to which the formal exigencies of a Christian work as such spontaneously tend; and I say that a work is in fact Christian so far as some element derived from the life which makes saints and contemplatives is transmitted—howsoever and with whatsoever deficiencies—through the soul of the artist.

These are self-evident truths, the simple application of the eternal principle: *operatio sequitur esse*, being is the measure of achievement. "That is the whole secret," said Goethe. "To be able *to do* something, you must *be* something." Leonardo illustrated this same principle by some curious observations: "A heavy-handed painter will make the hands heavy in his work and reproduce the defects of his body, unless he guards himself against this by prolonged study. . . . If he is a ready talker and of vivacious disposition, such also will his figures be. If the master is pious, his figures will have wry necks; if the master is lazy, they will express laziness to the life. . . . Every characteristic of painting is a characteristic of the painter" (Péladan's *Textes Choisis*, §§ 415, 422).

"How could artists of talent whose personal faith was pure and living—artists like Overbeck and certain pupils of Ingres—have produced works which hardly touch our religious sensibility?" asks Maurice Denis in an address on *Religious Sensibility in the Art of the Middle Ages* (*Nouvelles Théories*).

The answer is not far to seek. In the first place, it may well be that such lack of emotion proceeds simply from an insufficiency of the virtue of art, a very different thing from talent or school learning. In the second place, strictly speaking, the artist's faith and piety are not sufficient to make the work produce a Christian emotion: such a result always depends upon some element of contemplation, however inadequate, and contemplation itself presupposes, according to theologians, not only the virtue of faith, but also the influence of the gifts of the Holy Ghost. Lastly and above all, there may be, because of systematic school precepts, for example, obstacles, *prohibentia* preventing the art from being moved instrumentally and elevated by the whole soul. For in this case the virtue of art and the supernatural virtues of the Christian soul are not sufficient; the one must also be under the influence of the others. This takes place *naturally*, provided always that no alien element hinders. The religious emotion aroused by the Primitives is far from being the result of deliberate contrivance; it is a direct product of the ease and freedom with which these nurslings of Mother Church allowed their souls to pass into their art.

But how could artists so devoid of piety as many in the fourteenth and fifteenth centuries have produced works inspired by such intense religious feeling?

Such artists, in the first place however inclined to paganism they may be supposed to have been, were steeped in Faith as far as the mental structure of their being was concerned far more than our short-sighted psychology imagines. Were they not still close to the heart of those tumultuous and passionate, but still heroically Christian Middle Ages, whose imprint on our civilisation four centuries of modern culture have been unable to efface? They might abandon themselves to the coarsest forms of humour, but in their minds they still preserved, instinct with life, the *vis impressa* of the faith of the Middle Ages, and not of the faith only, but of those gifts of the Holy Ghost also which had been exercised with such fullness and freedom throughout the Christian centuries. So that it would not be rash to maintain that the "joyous livers" whom Maurice Denis quotes from Boccaccio found themselves in reality more "mystically" disposed before the work to be painted than many men of piety in our desiccated time.

In the second place, the *Christian quality* is just about to change in their works. Even before it became, in Raphael and earlier in Leonardo, pure humanity and pure nature, it had ceased, in Botticelli or Filippo Lippi, to be anything but sensitive grace. It preserved its serious and profound character only in the great Primitives, Cimabue, Giotto and Lorenzetti, or later in Angelico, who, because he was a saint, could transmit all the light of the interior heaven into an art already grown in itself less austere.

The truth is one has to go pretty far back into the Middle Ages, beyond the exquisite tenderness of St. Francis, to find the purest epoch of Christian art. When is there perfect harmony between a powerfully intellectual hieratic tradition—without which there can be no sacred art—and the free and ingenuous sense of reality which befits art under the law of liberty to be found more fully realised than in the sculptured figures and stained-glass windows of the cathedrals? No subsequent interpretation attains, for instance, the truly sacerdotal and theological elevation of the scenes of the Nativity of Our Lord (the Choir of Notre-Dame at Paris, the windows at Tours, Sens, Chartres, etc., *ponitur in praesepio, id est corpus Christi super altare*), or the Coronation of the Blessed Virgin (at Senlis), as they were conceived in the twelfth and thirteenth centuries (cf. Émile Male, *l'Art religieux du XIIIe siècle en France*; Dom Louis Baillet, *Le Couronnement de la Sainte Vierge*, Van Onzen Tijd, Afl. XII, 1910).

Again, art in those times was the fruit of a race moved by all the forces of Baptism. It is certainly right to insist on the *ingenuousness* of the Primitives and to attribute to such ingenuousness the emotion we experience before their works. But all great art is ingenuous, and not all great art is Christian, unless in hope. If the ingenuousness of our Primitives leads the heart to the living God, the reason is its unique quality; it is a *Christian* ingenuousness, an infused virtue of amazed ingenuousness and filial candour before the things created by the Holy Trinity, the peculiar character in art of the faith and the gifts transmitted to it and exalting it.

Because of this religious faith the Primitives knew by instinct what modern poetry has learned in suffering, "that form must be the form of the mind, the manner not of saying things but of thinking them"; and that "only reality, even carefully covered up, possesses the virtue of stirring the emotions" (Jean Cocteau, *Le Rappel à l'Ordre*).

For this reason also, in vain will M. Gaston Latouche maintain that the ceiling of the Chapel at Versailles strikes him as equally religious as the roof at Assisi: Jouvenet will continue not to exist by the side of Giotto so long as a sullen "classicist" fanaticism shall not have triumphed over the Christian heart.

The Russian philospher Berdiaeff maintains that a perfect classicism, that is to say a form capable of extracting from Nature an entirely happy and satisfying harmony, is impossible since the agony of Christ and His Crucifixion: according to him the classicism of the Renaissance retains without knowing it a Christian wound. I think Berdiaeff is right. But did perfect classical tranquillity ever exist even in Greece? A mysterious and sullen violence came breaking in upon that dream: for in Greece, too, human nature was wounded and craved for redemption.

136. "As the body of Jesus Christ was born of the chastity of the Virgin Mary by the Holy Ghost, even so is the praise of hymns in accordance with a heavenly harmony rooted in the Church through the Holy Ghost," writes St. Hildegarde in the admirable letter to the Chapter of Mainz claiming (and asserting) the liberty of sacred song (Migne, col. 221).

137. It is interesting to observe that contemporary art in its boldest researches seems to be anxious to attain everything which characterises primitive art in the construction of the work in the simplicity, candour, and rationality of the means, in the ideographical schematisation of expression. Consider from this angle the miniatures of the *Scivias* of St. Hildegarde reproduced in Dom Baillet's admirable work ("The Miniatures of the *Scivias* preserved in the Library of Wiesbaden," first fasc. of vol. xix of the *Monuments et Mémoires de l'Acad. des Insc. et Belles Lettres*, 1912), and many very suggestive analogies will be found with certain contemporary efforts—Cubist perspective, for example. But such analogies are all material; the inner principle is utterly different. What most "advanced" moderns are seeking in the cold night of a calculating anarchy, the Primitives possessed, without seeking, in the peace of interior order. Change the soul,

the inner principle, imagine the light of the Faith and reason taking the place of the exasperation of the senses (and sometimes even of *stultitia*), and you have an art capable of high spiritual developments. In that sense, although from other points of view it is diametrically opposed to Christianity, contemporary art is far closer to a Christian art than academic art.

137b. It goes without saying that the word "morality" must be understood not in the stoic, lay, or Protestant, sense, but in the Catholic sense, in which the order of morality or human conduct is completely determined by an end—the Beatific Vision and the love of God for His own sake and above all things—and grows to perfection in the supernatural life of the theological virtues and the gifts of the Spirit.

138. Here the testimony of a poet who was so jealous an artist as Baudelaire is of the highest interest. His essay on *The Pagan School*, vividly describing what an error it is for a man to address himself to art as his supreme end, concludes as follows: "The uncontrolled appetite for form impels the artist to monstrous, unknown disorders. Absorbed by the fierce passion for whatever is beautiful, comic, pretty or picturesque, for there are degrees, ideas of what is right and true disappear; the frenzied passion for art is a cancer which eats up everything else. And as the definite absence of what is right and true in art is tantamount to the absence of art, the man fades away completely: the excessive specialisation of a faculty ends in nothing. I can understand the rage of the iconoclasts and the Mohammedans against images. I admit all the remorse of St. Augustine for the overweening pleasure of the eyes. The danger is so great that I can forgive the suppression of the object. The folly of art is on a par with the abuse of the mind. The creation of one or other of these two supremacies begets stupidity, hardness of heart and unbound pride and egoism . . ." (Baudelaire, *L'Art romantique*).

139. St. Thomas, *Sum. Theol.*, ii–ii, q. 169, a. 2, *ad* 4. In this connection a familiar text of St. Thomas may be recalled. The Saint, commenting upon the *Ethics* of the philosopher, like him points out that it is for political science, as an architectonic science, to *give orders* to the "practical sciences," such as the mechanical arts, not only in the exercise of such sciences, but also in the very determination of the work (thus it orders the artisan who makes knives not merely to make use of his art, but to make use of it in such-and-such a way, by making such-and-such a

kind of knife: "both indeed are ordered to the end of human life."
Politics also gives orders to the speculative sciences, but only in
the exercise of such sciences, not in the determination of the work.
It prescribes that some shall teach, while others learn, geometry,
"such actions, so far as they are voluntary, relating in effect to the
matter of morality and being capable of being ordered to the
end of human life." But it does not prescribe to the geometer
what conclusions he shall come to concerning the triangle,
for that "is not of the province of human life and depends
only on the nature of things" (*Comment. in Ethic. Nicom.*, lib. i,
lect. 2).

St. Thomas does not mention the Fine Arts explicitly in this
passage, but it is not very difficult to apply such principles to
them, observing that they participate through the transcendence
of their object, which is beauty, in the nobility of the speculative
sciences—so that no *politicus* should dare meddle with the laws of
beauty—but they still remain, by their generic nature, arts,
"practical sciences," and on that score all the intellectual and
moral values the work absorbs normally come under the control
of whoever has the duty of taking care of the common good
of human life. Aristotle also adds that it is for Politics to use
for its own ends the noblest arts, such as the Military Art,
Economics, and Rhetoric.

140. *Met.*, xii, c. 10, 1075 a 15, St. Thomas, lect. 12. Cf. *Sum.
Theol.*, i–ii, q. 3, a. 5, *ad* 1.

141. "The good of an army is rather in the Commander than
in discipline: because in the matter of goodness the end is of
greater importance than things which are merely means to the
end. Now, discipline in the army is intended to fulfil the good of
the Commander, that is to say the will of the Commander in
winning a victory" (St. Thomas, commenting on the passage
quoted from Aristotle: *Ed. Cathala*, § 2630).

142. "It is by becoming national that a literature takes its
place in humanity and acquires significance in its assembly.
. . . What could be more Spanish than Cervantes, more English than Shakespeare, more Italian than Dante, more French
than Voltaire or Montaigne, Descartes or Pascal, what could be
more Russian than Dostoievsky; what is more universally human
than these?" (André Gide, *Réflexions sur l'Allemagne*.) "The
more a poet sings in his genealogical tree, the more his singing
is in tune." (Jean Cocteau.)

143. Of the people of Athens Charles Maurras has written: "The philosophical spirit, quickness to conceive the Universal, permeated all their arts, principally sculpture, poetry, architecture, and oratory. Once it yielded to this tendency, it put itself into perpetual communion with the human race. In the great classical days the dominant characteristic of all Greek art is simply intellectuality or humanity. The marvels which grew to perfection on the Acropolis thereby became the property, the model, and the sustenance, of all men: the classical, the Attic, is the more universal in proportion as it is more austerely Athenian—Athenian of an epoch and a taste better purged of all foreign influence. In the high moment when it was itself alone, Attica was the human race." It would appear that at the present time the French genius has a similar mission, but one compelling it to serve a more exalted universality than that of pure reason—the full catholicity of natural and supernatural truth.

144. St. Thomas, *in II Sent.*, d. 18, q. 2, 2.

145. *Sum. Theol.*, i–ii, q. 30, a. 4.

146. *Sum. Theol.*, ii–ii, q. 35, a. 4, *ad* 2. Cf. *Eth. Nic.*, viii, 5, 6; x, 6.

147. *Sum. Theol.*, i–ii, q. 3, a. 4.

148. "To this also (i.e. to contemplation) all other human operations seem to be ordered, as to an end; for soundness of body is required to make contemplation perfect and to soundness of body are ordered all the artificial necessaries of life. Tranquillity also is required from the perturbations of the passions; and this is attained through the moral virtues and prudence. Peace, too, from exterior passions; and to this the whole régime of civil life is ordered. So that all human functions, rightly considered, seem to be for the service of such as contemplate the truth" (*Sum. contra Gent.*, lib. iii, cap. 37, 6).

Such a doctrine enables one to appreciate the essential opposition, even in the order of ends, dividing the Christian from the modern State, which is orientated entirely towards practice, "production" and "consumption", not towards contemplation.

It is curious that a man like Wilde had realised "that while, in the opinion of society, contemplation is the gravest sin of which any citizen can be guilty, in the opinion of the highest culture it is the proper occupation of man" (*Intentions*, The Critic as

Artist, sixteenth Ed., pp. 170–1). But the unhappy man was nevertheless convinced that "we cannot go back to the saint," and that
"there is far more to be learned from the sinner"; which is a gross
absurdity, asserting that there is more in the less than in the more.
"It is enough that our fathers believed," thought Wilde. "They
have exhausted the faith-faculty of the species. . . . Who, as
Mr. Pater suggests somewhere, would exchange the curve of a
single rose-leaf for that formless intangible Being which Plato
rates so high?" In such a case the βίος θεωρητικός which was
his "true ideal" could only be æstheticism, the stupidest and most
mendacious caricature of contemplation; and he was compelled
to exert all his energies to establish his soul in that sham counterfeit of the intellectual life. In vain. In accordance with a fatal
law which I have described elsewhere (*Grandeur et Misère de la
Métaphysique*), incapable of rising to the love of God, he was
inevitably compelled to sink to the love below, under the influence
of his beloved Greeks, to become that terrible instrument of the
devil which has been so long the curse of modern literature.

149. *De. Div. Nomin.*, cap. iv.

150. *Exodus* xxxv. 30–5.

151. *Sum. Theol.*, i–ii, q. 43, a. 3. "When therefore a man gives
up using an intellectual habit, extraneous imaginations arise
which sometimes lead him the opposite way; so that if they are
not in a measure cut down or repressed by a frequent use of the
intellectual habit, the man becomes less fit to form a sound
judgement, and sometimes is wholly disposed the opposite way,
And so the intellectual habit through ceasing to be used becomes
less effective or even utterly spoiled."

152. *Ibid.*, q. 42, a. 3.

153. Jean Cocteau, *Le Coq et l'Arlequin*. "Be careful to
protect your virtue of working miracles, for if they knew you were
a missionary, they would pull your tongue out and your nails."

154. Hence so many conflicts between the prudent man and
the artist with regard to, e.g., the representation of the nude. One
member of an academy, concerned only with the subject represented, sees simply animality—and becomes rightly apprehensive for his own and his neighbour's. Another, concerned only
with the work itself, sees simply the formal aspect of beauty.

Maurice Denis (*Nouvelles Théories*) in this connection quotes the case of Renoir, rightly insisting on the lovely pictorial serenity of his figures. But such serenity did not preclude the artist himself from the possession of a lively sensuality of vision. (What should we say if Renoir were not in question, but that great faun-workman Rodin ?)

Whatever the state of this particular problem may be (the Middle Ages dealt with it severely, the Renaissance very generously, even in the matter of Church decoration), the fact still remains that, speaking generally, Catholicism alone is capable of reconciling perfectly Prudence and Art, because of the universality, the *catholicity* of its wisdom which embraces all reality. Therefore Protestants tax it with immorality and Humanists with rigorism, testifying alike to the superiority of its point of view.

As most men are not educated in any artistic culture, Prudence is right in being apprehensive of the effect on the masses of many works of art. And Catholicism, knowing that evil is to be encountered *ut in pluribus* in the human race, and yet obliged to concern itself with the good of the multitude, must in certain cases deny to art, in the name of the essential interests of the human being, liberties which art would jealously assert.

The "essential interest of the human being" here in question must be understood not only in relation to the passions of the flesh, but also in relation to the subject-matter of all the virtues, the integrity of the mind first of all—not to mention the interests of art itself, and the need it has of being protected by the discipline of religion against the dissolution of everything there is in man.

It is difficult no doubt in such a case to preserve the balance. At all events to be frightened of art, to flee from it and put it to flight, is certainly no solution. There is a superior wisdom in trusting as much as possible to the powers of the mind. It is desirable that Catholics in our day should remember that the Church alone has succeeded in forming the people on beauty, protecting them the while against the "corruption" which Plato and Rousseau ascribe to art and poetry. The spirit of Luther, Jean-Jacques or Tolstoi has no place amongst us: if we defend the rights of God in the order of moral good, we defend them also in the order of intelligence and beauty, and nothing compels us to go on all fours for the love of virtue. Every time he finds in a Christian environment a contempt for intelligence or art, that is to say for truth and beauty, we may be sure that the devil scores a point.

I do not overlook the necessity for prohibitive measures. Human frailty makes them indispensable: it must be protected. It is none the less clear that prohibitive measures, however necessary they may be, remain by nature less effective and less important than a robust intellectual and religious training, enabling mind and heart to resist *vitally* any morbid principle.

As for the freedom of the artist with regard to the subjects he is to represent, the problem seems to be as a rule badly stated, because it is forgotten that the subject is merely the matter of the work of art. The essential question is not to know whether a novelist can or cannot depict such-and-such an aspect of evil. The essential question is *from what altitude* he depicts it and whether his art and mind are pure enough and strong enough to depict it without connivance. The more deeply the modern novel probes human misery, the more does it require superhuman virtues in the novelist. To write Proust's work as it asked to be written would have required the inner light of a St. Augustine. Alas ! It is the opposite which happens, and we see the observer and the thing observed, the novelist and his subject, rivals in a competition to degrade. From this point of view the influence of André Gide on French literature must be considered as very characteristic. The way in which he has surpassed himself in his latest books confirms the judgement passed on him by Massis.

I have mentioned the novel. The novel differs from other forms of literature in having for object not the manufacture of something with its own special beauty in the world of *artefacta*, deriving only its elements from human life, but the conduct of human life itself in fiction, like providential art in reality. The object it has to create is human life itself; it has to mould, scrutinise and govern humanity. Such seems to me to be the distinctive characteristic of the art of the novel.[1] (I mean the modern novel of which Balzac is the father. Its fundamental difference from the novel of antiquity has been rightly pointed out by Ernest Hello in an essay which in other respects is rhetorical: the novel of the Ancients was above all a voyage into the marvellous and the *ideal*, a deliverance of the imagination.)

It may therefore be understood how honest, authentic and universal the novelist's realism ought to be: only a Christian, nay a mystic, because he has some idea of *what there is in man*, can be a complete novelist. "There is not," said Georges Bernanos with reference to Balzac, "a single feature to add to any one of his frightful characters, but he has not been down to the secret spring, the innermost recesses of conscience, where evil organises from within, against God and for the love of death, that

[1] Cf. Henri Massis, *Réflexions sur l'art du roman.* (Paris, Plon, 1926.) Frédéric Lefèvre, *Georges Bernanos.* (Paris, La Tour d'Ivoire, 1926.)

part of us the harmony of which has been destroyed by original sin. . . ." And again: "Take the characters of Dostoievsky, those whom he himself calls *The Possessed*. We know the diagnosis of the great Russian in regard to them. But what would have been the diagnosis of a Curé d'Ars, for instance? What would he have seen in those obscure souls?"[1]

155. Cf. *Sum. Theol.*, i–ii, q. 66, a. 3; ii–ii, q. 47, a. 4.

156. Cf. *Sum. Theol.*, i–ii, q. 66, a. 3, *ad.* 1. "The fact that the moral virtues are more necessary to human life does not prove that they are nobler *simpliciter*, but only *quoad hoc*. The intellectual speculative virtues, by the very fact of their not being ordered to another purpose, as the useful is ordered to the end it serves, are worthier. . . ."

157. *Eth. Nic.*, x. 8; cf. *Sum. Theol.*, ii–ii, q. 47, a. 15.

158. *Sum. Theol.*, i–ii, q. 66, a. 5.

159. Cf. the observations of the learned theologian Arintero, O.P., in his treatise *Cuestiones misticas* (Salamanca, 1916), and above all P. Garrigou-Lagrange's *Perfection chrétienne et contemplation* (Saint-Maximin, 1923).

160. Criticism, on the other hand, though it can always derive its inspiration from philosophical principles—always a good thing, but risky—remains on the same plane as the work and the particular, without being itself operative or making any creative judgement, rather judging from without and after the event. Therefore Wilde made a gross mistake in placing the critic above the artist, although he might have invoked the testimony of Plutarch, who says somewhere, if my memory does not fail me, "Would anyone given the choice, not rather enjoy the contemplation of the work of Phidias than be Phidias himself?"

161. Some critics have gently reproached me for having omitted to mention the Spanish and Jesuit Baroque, which they rightly admire. But there are many more important examples, both in Byzantium and the Far East, which I have not pressed into service.

162. John of St. Thomas, *Curs. Theol.* (Vivès, t. iii), q. xv, *de ideis*, disp. 1, a. 1, §13. "Many people see perfectly and know

[1] Frédéric Lefèvre, *op. cit.*

an object of artistic production, e.g. a horse or a statue; and natural things also are perfectly known by many people. Nevertheless they have no *idea* of such things, because they are not artisans, still less makers of natural things. Now, an idea is the constructive form of that of which the object of the idea is an example."

163. "For truth of this sort is one of the boundaries of this world: it is forbidden to establish yourself there. Nothing so pure can coexist with the conditions of life" (Paul Valéry, Preface to Lucien Fabre's *Connaissance de la Déesse.*)

164. A similar antinomy is implicit in all things which (like the mind and art) touch the transcendental order and are realised either in a pure state in God or "by participation" in created subjects. As they tend (with an ineffective tendency which is none the less real) to the fullness of their essence *considered in itself* (transcendentally) *and in its pure formal line,* so they tend to surpass themselves, to cross the boundaries of their essence *considered in a created subject* (with the specific determinations there appropriate to it), and in so doing to escape from their *conditions of existence.*

So the mind tends in the case of man, in whom it is reason, to rejoin the perfection of its essence transcendentally considered, and thereby to go beyond its boundaries as reason, and its conditions of existence in the subject. Hence, if grace does not intervene to elevate nature, the angelic swoon into an "abstract intellection," which then becomes a mystical suicide of thought.

165. "'Poetry is theology,' says Boccaccio in his commentary upon the *Divina Commedia.* Ontology would perhaps be the better name, for poetry inclines above all to the roots of the knowledge of Being" (Charles Maurras, Preface to *La Musique Intérieure*).

166. Cf. St. Thomas Aquinas, *Comment. in Eth. Nicom.,* lib. i, lect. 2 (cf. Note 139).

167. Charles Maurras.

168. Henri Ghéon lately stressed the advantage for artists of such a conception of the world as would "reinstate them in the social body," and "keep the common circulation running

through them, without which neither art nor society can breathe or nourish itself" (Preface to *Partis Pris*).

169. Cf. Pierre Reverdy, *Nord-Sud*, Nos. 4, 5, 8, 13.

170. Even those who to-day derive their inspiration from Rimbaud do not so much continue his poetry in the line of art as transpose it into the line of moral life and action. The influence of Lautréamont, which here mingles with that of Rimbaud, alike affects the sphere of moral and metaphysical life more than the sphere of art. Touching *Chants de Maldoror*, it may be pertinently observed that, as early as 1887, Léon Bloy in *Le Désespéré* proclaimed the historical importance of these "good tidings of *damnation*," noting in them "one of the least ambiguous signs that the modern generation had been brought to bay at the extremity of all things." It was he who wrote of Lautréamount with the deepest understanding (in an article written in 1890 and republished in *Belluaires et Porchers*).

171. Cf. St. Thomas, *Sum. Theol.*, i, q. 19, a. 1, *ad* 3.

172. Paul Claudel, "Introd. à un poème sur Dante," *Correspondant*, September 10, 1921.

173. The phrase *subjection to the object*, which is perfectly clear as far as science is concerned, easily becomes obscure when referred to art. For the formal object of art is not a thing to which to conform, but a thing to form. To say that art ought to be subjected to the object is then to say that it ought to be subjected *to the object to be made as such* or to the undeviating rules of operation through which that object will well and truly be what it ought to be. (Academicism with its formulas, pseudo-classicism with its clichés and its mythology, Hugotism and Wagnerism with their worship of the word and effect, all fail so to subject themselves.)

Materially speaking—taking into consideration not the formal object of the art but its material object, the reality whose image it transmits into the work—the submission to such an object ought to be understood in a hundred different ways and precisely according to the formal object of the artist in each particular case. In the case of the novel it would not be unfair to criticise Flaubert with Cocteau, for his *style as a starting-point* or, with Ghéon, for his *indifference to the subject*. In the case of the prose poem as Max Jacob has defined it, it is, on the contrary, the construction of the poem which will constitute the whole object of the art, and the subject ought to intervene only in an indirect and material way.

174. Arthur Rimbaud, *Une saison en enfer*.

175. "So to simplify things, let us call this fluid 'poetry' and art the more or less felicitous exercise by which it is controlled and made serviceable." Jean Cocteau, *Le Rappel à l'Ordre* (Le Secret Professionnel). Cocteau's book contains observations of the utmost value on this question of art and poetry.

176. I am not in the least thinking here of the pursuit of abstract poetry in the Mallarméan sense, of poetry as an *abstract art* which would "result, by a kind of *exhaustion*, from the progressive suppression of all the prose elements in a poem" (Paul Valéry, ap. Frédéric Lèfevre, *Entretiens*). I have in mind rather the pursuit of the *poetic spirit* in a pure state, that is to say something utterly different and ever so much more profound, a whole region of metaphysics still unexplored.

177. Jean Cocteau, *Le Rappel à l'Ordre* (Le Secret Professionnel; Picasso). Cf. Pierre Reverdy, *Pablo Picasso*.

178. André Breton, *Les Pas perdus*.

179. Demonologists are well aware that every *passive condition into which man puts himself* is a door opened to the devil.

180. Jean Cocteau, *Orphée*.

181. The history of the theatre offers a particularly striking example of this, as was recently observed by Henri Ghéon in his lectures at the Vieux-Colombier and by Gaston Baty in his book, *Le Masque et l'Encensoir*.

182. Max Jacob, *Art poétique*.

183. Cf. Paul Claudel, "Réflexions et Propositions sur le vers français, Parabole d'Animus et d'Anima," *Nouv. Rev. Franç.*, October and November 1925: Claudel explained and limited the meaning of this fable in a letter to P. de Tonquèdec (*Études* October 20, 1926).

184. Léon Bloy, *La Femme Pauvre*. ["There is another still," adds Judith Érèbe, "not even to be sorrowful at not wishing to be a saint" (*Roseau d'Or*, Fourth Series, 8th Cahier, Plon, 1929).]

185. In practice, printing and modern methods of vulgarisation, by confusing different publics more and more in one shapeless mass, run the risk of making a problem already singularly difficult well-nigh insoluble.

186. "When you've got the man you can judge the work, when you've got the work you can judge the man. Just think, if one of them is good, what the other could be" (Pierre Reverdy, *Self-Defence*).

187. Cf. Henri Massis, "Littérature et Catholicisme" (in *Réflexions sur l'art du roman*).

188. Plotinus, *Enneades*, i, 4.

189. Max Jacob, *Art poétique*.

190. Nietzsche, *The Case of Wagner*.

191. "Saint Theresa of Lisieux said, '*I prefer sacrifice to any ecstasy.*' A poet ought to have these words tattooed upon his heart" (Jean Cocteau, *Lettre à Jacques Maritain*).

192. Oscar Wilde, *De Profundis*.

193. Paul Claudel, "Lettre à Alexandre Cingria sur la décadence de l'art sacré," *Revue des Jeunes*, August 25, 1929.

194. Guillaume Apollinaire, "Les Collines" (*Calligrammes*).

195. Julien Lanoë, "Trois siècles de littérature," *La Ligne de Cœur*, June 25, 1926.

196. John of St. Thomas, *Curs. Theol.*, q. xxvii, disp. 12, a. 6, § 21 (Vivès, t. iv). On the other hands according to Plotinus, generation is a mark of indigence (ἔνδεια). "Anyone who has no desire to engender is the more completely self-sufficient in beauty: the desire to produce beauty proceeds from the absence of self-sufficiency and from the hope of obtaining greater satisfaction by producing and engendering in beauty" (*Enneades*, iii, 5, 1,

46–9, περὶ ἐρῶτος). This aspect of indigence bound to transitive activity is the price we have to pay for our condition
of material beings, but does not essentially affect (therein lies the
error of the neo-Platonic metaphysics) the engendering fecundity
itself, which in the immanent activity peculiar to life is above
all superabundance—particularly as a more exalted, more
immaterial form of life is here involved.

197. Max Jacob, *Art poétique*.

Printed in the United States
1522200001B/391-392